Knowing Christ

Christian Discipleship and the Eucharist

— DAVID R. TOMLINSON —

Sacristy
Press

Sacristy Press
PO Box 612, Durham, DH1 9HT

www.sacristy.co.uk

First published in 2020 by Sacristy Press, Durham

Copyright © David R. Tomlinson 2020
The moral rights of the author have been asserted

All rights reserved, no part of this publication may be reproduced or transmitted in any form or by any means, electronic, mechanical photocopying, documentary, film or in any other format without prior written permission of the publisher.

Scripture quotations, unless otherwise stated, are from the *New Revised Standard Version Bible: Anglicized Edition*, copyright © 1989, 1995 National Council of the Churches of Christ in the United States of America. Used by permission. All rights reserved worldwide.

Material from *Common Worship: Services and Prayers for the Church of England* is © The Archbishops' Council 2000. Published by Church House Publishing. Used by permission. rights@hymnsam.co.uk

Every reasonable effort has been made to trace the copyright holders of material reproduced in this book, but if any have been inadvertently overlooked the publisher would be glad to hear from them.

Sacristy Limited, registered in England & Wales, number 7565667

British Library Cataloguing-in-Publication Data
A catalogue record for the book is available from the British Library

ISBN 978-1-78959-122-4

Contents

Introduction 1

Part 1 7
1. Love 9
2. Death and resurrection 19
3. Do this in remembrance of me. 33
4. The Holy Spirit 42
5. Living eucharistically 48
6. Communion 63
7. Seeing Christ in everyday life 68
8. Looking for the coming of the kingdom. 77

Part 2 83
9. Gathering. 85
10. Purity of heart. 93
11. Penitence 98
12. Praise and worship 103
13. Praying silently 109
14. The Word. 112
15. Believing 122
16. Interceding 126
17. The Body of Christ 132
18. The Eucharistic Prayer 140
19. Our Father 150
20. Being fed 154
21. Going 160

Epilogue: The Eucharist in a time of pandemic 170

Bibliography 176
Notes 179

Introduction

I think my first stirrings of a conscious commitment to Christ were at my school when I was about seven years old. As my faith in God began to take shape, it appeared that I had been offered an opportunity to eat the bread and drink the wine of the Eucharist. That offer was then taken away.

My father had been seconded to the World Health Organization in Copenhagen for a year and had taken his family with him. I was enrolled at the Roman Catholic English-speaking school in Copenhagen and embraced the school's religiosity; I remember crossing myself every morning as I came through the arched entrance over which there was a crucifix. When my class was invited to consider joining the preparation course for "admission to the sacrament of Holy Communion", I was keen to proceed with most of my classmates. I was mystified when I was told that I could not because I was a "Protestant". I was disappointed and could make no sense of why I was barred. Even at this early stage, I felt that I had missed out on something special and, looking back, now realize that this was a setback on my journey of faith. It was not until my teenage years that I began to ask questions about Christianity and to explore my faith again.

In my final year at university, I committed my life to Christ in the time between Christmas and New Year's Eve and was baptized and confirmed two years later. My joy at my baptism and admission to Holy Communion fulfilled my journey of faith so far, and renewed my discipleship.

When training for ordination, I was surprised by the lack of teaching on the liturgy of the Eucharist. Whatever the reason, it still seems a serious omission. I would have found some instruction on each element of the liturgy and an explanation of how they fit together helpful. Over the years since, I have carried out my own research and found it rewarding. This book is the fruit of that work. I remain, though, curious about the

Eucharist, and aware that there will always be a sense of mystery about it as there is about God, and always more to discover.

I hope to add to the reader's appreciation of this central act of Christian worship and thereby deepen their understanding of what it means to be a disciple of Christ. The connection between the Eucharist and discipleship is my recurring theme: I believe that the Eucharist defines Christian discipleship and is the supreme way by which we are taken further into the mystery of Christ. By celebrating the Eucharist, we know Christ and learn how to live for him.

I have decided to use the term "Eucharist", rather than the other options, as it is based on the Greek word *eucharistia*, which means "thanksgiving", and I value how this defines humanity primarily as the recipient of God's good gifts: God is the Giver and we respond with thanksgiving. If you are more used to another name for the service, then simply read "Eucharist" as referring to that name. I have referred to the act of leading the celebration of the Eucharist as 'presiding' and, correspondingly, described the leader as the 'president'.

Each chapter begins with a quotation and an introduction. When these are personal stories, I have sometimes changed the names to protect anonymity.

I hope that as well as enriching your experience of the Eucharist, you will be drawn closer to Christ by reading this book. As it is designed to be devotional as well as informative, I end each chapter with a prayer.

This book is in two parts. In the first eight chapters, I explore what I see as the foundational ideas for an understanding of the Eucharist. The rest of the book is a journey through the liturgy, drawing upon *Common Worship*, one of the two authorized Church of England books of services and prayers.

In the first chapter, I identify the Eucharist as the supreme setting in which we experience and respond to God's love, revealed in Jesus Christ, and in sharp focus on the cross.

Through baptism, we are plunged into the Paschal Mystery, the death and resurrection of Christ. Dying and rising with Christ is at the heart of Christian discipleship, and gives us confidence in the face of our mortality. This is the subject of the second chapter.

From the "gathering" to the "sending out", the whole Eucharist is an act of remembrance, and this is the focus of chapter 3. When we obey Jesus' command, "Do this in remembrance of me", we are not so much recalling the past as participating anew in the central events of the Christian faith. What is true of the Eucharist is true of every other facet of life for the disciple of Christ; we seek to be mindful of Christ and to share in Christ's life.

In chapter 4, I highlight the essential role of the Holy Spirit in the Eucharist and in our discipleship. In the power of the Spirit, we celebrate the Eucharist and live for God.

Paul's encouragement to the church in Thessalonica to "rejoice always, pray without ceasing, give thanks in all circumstances" is the topic of chapter 5. By letting the Eucharist shape our lives, we learn to be a rejoicing, praying and thankful people. As we live eucharistically, we fulfil "the will of God in Christ Jesus" (1 Thessalonians 5:16–18).

In the Eucharist, we experience communion with God and with each other. Our closeness to God and the depth of our shared life in our churches are interrelated. By participating in God's life, we are drawn closer together. By loving each other, we are taken further into the life of God. This dynamic is transformational, as I explore in chapter 6.

Through our intimate encounter with God in the Eucharist, we learn to meet Christ in everyday life. We receive the sacrament—the bread and wine that are to us the body and blood of Christ—so that the rest of life becomes sacramental, a means of knowing and relating to God, as we see in chapter 7.

Reflection on the connection between the kingdom of God and the Eucharist in chapter 8 brings the first part of the book to a close. Our eating and drinking in the Eucharist are an anticipation of the end of time: when the kingdom of God comes, there will be a feast.

In part 2, I have followed the pattern of the Eucharist in the Church of England's *Common Worship* known as *Order One*. As we journey through the Eucharist from the people assembling to being dismissed, I consider in turn the key elements of the service. In chapter 9, I start with the "gathering" and the definition of the Church as a people called out from the world to come together to worship.

In the prayer known as the *Collect for Purity*, we ask God to "cleanse the thoughts of our hearts". As our hearts are purified, our eyes our opened and we see God (Matthew 5:8). Our openness to God's transforming work in our lives is vital to our growth in faith, and is the subject of chapter 10.

The cross demonstrates both our resistance to God and God's eternal love. When we are confident in God's love for us, we can be honest with God about our sins. Our prayers of penitence are our response to the cross of Christ, as we consider in chapter 11.

In extolling the greatness of God, as we do through the *Gloria in Excelsis Deo*, we see ourselves, our lives and our world in their true perspective. Since we are created to worship God, we fulfil our eternal purpose by joining in this great hymn of praise. This is the focus in chapter 12.

After the *Gloria*, there is a time set aside for silent prayer which is followed by the Collect, the prayer that gathers what is offered in the stillness and presents it to God. Praying in silence is the subject of chapter 13.

Next, we move on to the Ministry of the Word in chapter 14: God speaks to us through the Bible readings and the sermon. Whilst we know Christ through all the Scriptures, we pay particular attention to the Gospels, where we hear the words and actions of his incarnate life. I also outline the preacher's task, and stress the importance of engagement with the Bible in our daily discipleship.

In the next two chapters, we move from declaring our faith together to the prayers of intercession. After the sermon, we recite a creed. By publicly affirming our faith, we strengthen our confidence in God. Having expressed our faith in God, we intercede for God's Church and world. In our prayers, we hold before us the vision of God's kingdom of justice and peace, align ourselves with God's loving purposes, and share in Christ's intercession.

In chapter 17, the exchange of the Peace with our brothers and sisters in Christ in the service leads on to an exploration of what it means for the Church to be the Body of Christ.

We move from the Eucharistic Prayer to the Lord's Prayer through chapters 18 and 19. Eucharistic Prayer B in *Common Worship* is derived from the third-century liturgy of Hippolytus. It reflects the classic structure and features of the Church's central prayer of thanksgiving, the Eucharistic Prayer. I take us through it and give some insights into its meaning. As we pray the Lord's Prayer, we participate in the Son's relationship with the Father. In the Eucharist, when we say these familiar and familial words, we are in the Father's presence.

In the Eucharist, eating bread and drinking wine meets our hunger for God, yet it also reminds us of our physical hunger. "Being fed" is the topic of chapter 20.

At the end of the Eucharist, the Church is sent out into the world to collaborate with God in God's mission. I use the Anglican Consultative Council's Five Marks of Mission as a reference point in chapter 21.

I have also included an epilogue on the Eucharist in the lockdown caused by the COVID-19 pandemic. I offer some reflections on how the Church is responding to this crisis, and particularly on the celebration of the Eucharist when there can be no services in church. This additional chapter rounds off the book.

When I have given "Church" an initial capital letter, it refers to the whole Church, the global body of Christians. When it begins with a lower-case letter, it denotes a local church.

When I refer to the "End" this relates to the consummation of God's intention for creation. When the kingdom of God comes to earth, then time will have reached its fulfilment. There will be no more tears, death or pain (Revelation 21:4). The earth will be filled with the knowledge of the glory of God (Habakkuk 2:14). This is the "End" for which we pray.

I would like to thank Jill Hrouda and Clifford Want for proofreading the text, and Jenny Tomlinson for her observations about the style and content.

I am also grateful to all the churches where I have celebrated the Eucharist, especially those where I have been privileged to preside. In the exchange at the start of the Eucharistic Prayer, when the president says "Lift up your hearts" and the congregation responds with "We lift them to the Lord", I have felt the joy and known the privilege of leading this great prayer of thanksgiving. I increasingly appreciate the Eucharist as the culmination and source of a church's common life. Out of our encounter with the Risen Christ in the Eucharist, our discipleship flows.

I would like to dedicate this book to the Community of the Servants of God in Crawley Down. As I have worshipped in the chapel there, I have learned much about the Eucharist. It is also where I first heard and read that to follow Christ faithfully is to live a eucharistic life.

Part 1

CHAPTER 1

Love

We have known and believe the love that God has for us. God is love, and those who abide in love abide in God, and God abides in them.
1 John 4:16

In his book *Love's Endeavour, Love's Expense*, W. H. Vanstone seeks to define love though he acknowledges it is far from an easy task. He starts by drawing attention to the overuse of this word, "love": we use it too easily and so cheapen its value. Yet, he reckons that we all know the "real thing" when we find it. However, putting our experience into words by trying to cite love's distinctive features is a different matter. Since giving a full description of love is even harder, he tries instead to identify how we know when what is presented as love does not match up to our expectations. What is it about a relationship that signals to us that what is professed as love is inauthentic? He identifies three markers—control, detachment, and limit—that tell us that what is offered is an imitation and does not measure up. When these three features are absent, then there is love. Let me explain further.

The first authenticating feature of love is an absence of control. When the lover seeks in any way to control the beloved, we know that this relationship is marred by a lack of freedom. For love to flourish, the lover needs to give the beloved the space to respond freely. We know that love cannot be forced, and attempts to demand love from someone fail instantly. The act of putting someone under pressure to love is a contradiction and by its nature makes love impossible.

The second authenticating characteristic of love is an absence of detachment. If the lover is detached, not affected by the beloved's suffering or joy, then the relationship looks cold and distant; there is not love. For there to be love, the lover must empathize with the beloved. When the beloved laughs, the lover laughs too. When the beloved weeps, the lover also sheds tears.

The third authenticating characteristic of love is an absence of limit. When the lover places limits on their love for the beloved, refusing to do this or that for the beloved because it is too demanding or too costly, then we know what is on offer is lacking, and does not deserve to be defined as "love".

By identifying these three markers of love's absence—control, detachment, and limit—Vanstone works his way towards a positive portrayal of love. Given that there must be an absence of control, the lover gives the beloved the freedom to respond, for love cannot be coerced. It must be offered freely and freely received, and what is more, love is liberating for both the beloved and the lover; they are set free to be more themselves. The lover is not aloof, removed from the beloved's feelings and mood, but profoundly responsive. What the beloved feels, the lover experiences too. The lover identifies with the beloved. Since there are no limits to love, there is nothing that the lover will not do for the beloved. Often, we discover this truth in the very act of loving. As we love, we discover, sometimes to our surprise, the depths of our love, and find our hearts enlarging—the scope of our love expanding.

When I ask parents preparing for their child's baptism, "What has surprised you about being a parent?" they often answer that they had no idea, before the birth, how much they would love their child and how now they would do anything for them. The sleepless nights, the nappy changing, and the general reorientation of life around the child are costly, and are all an expression of this new-found, sometimes overwhelming love. David Schwimmer, the actor most famous for playing Ross Geller in the American sitcom *Friends*, was astounded by the scale of his love for his daughter, as he discovered a capacity to love way beyond his previous experience. "I don't think that I've ever loved unconditionally before—even with partners, lovers. I think that there has always been a part of me that would hold back in some way. Now I realize that it is like part of me kind of cracked open. My heart is bigger than I ever thought that it was."[1] Like everyone who loves, he realized the intensity of his love in what he was prepared to do for the one he loved. It is in the sacrifices we make and in how much of ourselves we give that we discover how strong our love is. Our love is expressed most eloquently in what it costs us.

God's love exemplifies supremely the three defining features of love identified by Vanstone. God gives us the space to respond freely to God's love: we are not controlled but set free to receive and return God's love if we choose. Yes, God knocks at the door of our lives, but only we can open it (Revelation 3:20). Opened up to God's love, we are liberated to become the people God created us to be.

Far from detached, God is intimately involved in our lives. Besides our life and our continued existence being dependent on the sustaining action of God, God is deeply engaged in our lives, even empathizing with us. When we grieve, God mourns; when we are happy, God celebrates. God's love is infinite, boundless and eternal, stretching through and beyond time.

In the gift of God's Son, we see the immeasurable nature of God's love and know that nothing can ever separate us from "God's love in Christ Jesus" (Romans 8:31–9). God's love is exemplified sharply and vividly in the unsurpassable symbol of love: the death of Jesus Christ on the cross.

The cross—the stretched-out love of God

On the evening before Jesus' crucifixion, as he shared a last meal with his friends, he embraced his forthcoming death, accepting the pain and suffering to come. Jesus spoke these words over the bread and wine: "This is my body broken for you" and "This is my blood shed for you". The bread—torn in two and distributed—and the wine—poured out into a common cup and drunk—spoke of a body broken and of blood shed for them. We can imagine how the disciples must have felt. Perhaps a strange mixture of confusion—what did he mean?—and foreboding—whatever was about to happen next seemed ominous and heavy with significance.

When Jesus offers the bread and wine to God, breaks the bread and pours out the wine, he assents to all that is about to happen. This decisive moment is central to the celebration of the Eucharist. As he ventures out into the darkness of the night—metaphorically as well as literally dark—he is ready for what will unfold.

Every Eucharistic Prayer—the climactic prayer of thanksgiving in the Eucharist—refers back to this last meal that Jesus had with his friends. The pathos of this night is captured in the stark "institution narrative." It is based on a passage from Paul's first letter to the church in Corinth:

> For I received from the Lord what I also handed on to you, that the Lord Jesus on the night when he was betrayed took a loaf of bread, and when he had given thanks, he broke it and said, "This is my body that is for you. Do this in remembrance of me." In the same way, he took the cup also, after supper, saying, "This cup is the new covenant in my blood. Do this, as often as you drink it, in remembrance of me."
>
> *1 Corinthians 11:23–5*

There are several variations on how this night is described in the Eucharistic Prayer, such as "On the night before he died . . . " and "On the night he was betrayed . . . " but the phrase that best captures the import of this decisive moment is, "On the night that he gave himself up . . . ". Each time we recall that night, we remember that when Jesus broke the bread and poured out the wine, he resolved to give himself for us on the cross.

The cross—God's love and our sin

As we contemplate the cross, we become aware of the generosity of God's love and the cost of our sin. These two realities are integral to this one event, for in the death of Christ, we know God's love—its height, depth and breadth—and what overcoming our resistance to God—our sin—has cost God.

In the Old Testament, we read of how God's people struggled to learn to love God. When they enjoyed military success and prospered, they became complacent, paid only lip service to God, and lost sight of justice. When subjugated by other nations, they were unfaithful and worshipped the gods of the dominant culture. It was through times of testing—in the wilderness, in exile, in drought and famine—that they repented and returned to God, rediscovering what it meant to be God's people, and experienced renewal.

God's people are called to love God as God loves them, unconditionally, with no ifs or buts. To love God whatever the circumstances, whether life is easy or hard, is a challenge. In aspiring to love God in this way, Israel moved forwards and then backwards, progressing and regressing, but gradually the nation's understanding of God, and the depth of her faith, deepened. Israel's story reveals a long and chequered struggle to match God's faithfulness to them; it is a narrative in which we do see some examples of this mature love for God when God is loved despite calamity and in crisis (Habakkuk 3:17–19). Ultimately though, the nation's calling to love God fully is fulfilled by God's Messiah, the Christ, who loves God from birth to death. Even in his death, he offers himself to God unreservedly and with inexhaustible confidence.

Besides his death being the climax of an obedient life, his final breath is the culmination too of humanity's striving to respond to God's overtures of love. As he is lifted on the cross at Calvary, Jesus scales the summit of love. If we imagine Jesus' journey through life as a mountain climb with steep slopes, crevasses to cross and boulders to circumvent, in his death, he finally approaches the peak, having successfully negotiated each preceding test of love. This high point is humanity's supreme response to God's love; this is the definitive act of love, never to be superseded.

As our representative, Christ responds to God's love as the whole of humanity is summoned to do. In giving his life, he demonstrates and consummates his love for God. Paradoxically, at the same time, he plumbs the depths of humanity's resistance to God, yet stays steadfastly faithful. Through Jesus' climactic surrender to God's love in his death, humanity is reshaped and reformed, and a new humanity is born. His letting go of his life is our liberation. We are forgiven and set free, and invited to share Christ's life and love for God.

Jesus' utter obedience to the first commandment to "love the Lord your God with all your heart, and with all your soul, and with all your might" leads to his death and our salvation (Deuteronomy 6:5). God's judgement on humanity's disobedience is disclosed, and the debt of our sin is paid, as this life is offered and received (Romans 3; 1 John 2). Jesus' cry on the cross, "It is finished", signals his work is complete (John 19:30).

In self-giving love, God in Christ restores and fulfils God's relationship with humanity, and we are forgiven.

We are urged to respond to Christ's grace and mercy by loving God unswervingly, whatever life brings. In his sacrificial love for God, Jesus realizes humanity's purpose: to love God with the same passion that God loves us. Having achieved this goal, Jesus draws us into a renewed humanity now capable of loving as Christ loves. This is the Christian gospel: we are invited to know Christ, and to share in Christ's love for humanity and for our heavenly Father.

We pray with Jesus, " . . . your will be done" (Matthew 26:42)

Jesus wrestles with the Father in prayer in the Garden of Gethsemane. Three times, he searches the Father's heart to see if there is an alternative to arrest and crucifixion: "My Father, if it is possible, let this cup pass from me; yet not what I want but what you want" (Matthew 26:39). At the end of this struggle, Jesus once more commits himself to the Father's will. In line with the Father's and Son's unity of will and purpose, Jesus then goes to meet those who have come to arrest him, including Judas Iscariot, his betrayer.

By his loving submission to God, Jesus heals our humanity. We are created to love but our humanity is shrivelled by selfishness. By his unfailing obedience, even to death on the cross, Jesus renews our humanity, aligning our intentions with the Father's heart, and making us holy. In Christ, we participate in the Son's relationship of love with the Father, and yearn with Christ for the Father's will to be done.

Since the Son finds in the Father the centre of his existence, his will is the same as the Father's. This finds expression in the plea Jesus taught his disciples to pray, "Your will be done", which he prayed intensely in the Garden of Gethsemane. While the Son eternally gives his life to the Father, the cross is the historical and definitive expression of his self-offering.

In the Eucharist, the Church beholds the Son's offering of himself on the cross. We see its costliness and yet are drawn into it. Taken deeper into Christ's self-giving love each time we celebrate the Eucharist, our love for the Father and for all the Father loves, the whole of creation, flourishes and matures. As our desires and plans more faithfully reflect God's purposes, we learn to pray with increasing fervour and mounting conviction "Your will be done."

Only by loving God can we know God

Since God is love, it is God's will that we love each other. Indeed, it is in loving each other that we imitate God and participate in God's life. When we love, our lives resonate with God's life and we know that God is with us. "If we love one another, God lives in us, and his love is perfected in us" (1 John 4:12).

God is the spring and source of love, and continuing the aquatic imagery, we can compare enjoying God's love to time spent paddling in a warm sea. Let us picture the Mediterranean Sea in the summer, and imagine that when we love, we leave the beach and venture into the shallows. This vision of splashing around in the sea together, joined by the water around us that is always there, reminds us too that our love for each other is a sharing in the communion, the eternal love, of Father, Son and Holy Spirit. The triune God is the locus of this closeness to each other. Our unity in love is derived from our intimate relationship with God. Through this unified life, that is God's and has become ours in Christ, the Church offers love to the world. As we learn to serve each other, we model an alternative to competitive modes of relating that cause rivalry and disharmony. By loving each other, we offer an alternative way of being together to our locality and the wider world, which is often blighted by division and enmity. We are to undermine society's increasing tribalism by transcending it in our common life. Each community centred on Christ is to embody the unity at the heart of God.

The Church is to exemplify God's comprehensive love to a fractured world. God's love draws people together from across the range of human diversity into one global community. God's intention is to bring the whole of humanity and the entire creation into harmony: nothing and no-one is excluded from God's loving purpose to unite the whole of creation in Christ. For the Church, this means that there can be no limit to our concern. We are summoned to care across national and continental boundaries. As our compassion is to stretch around the world, we have to be troubled by the degradation of the planet and the damage wreaked by climate change. Droughts, storms and heatwaves have a disproportionate impact on the poorer nations, and rising sea levels even put some nations' survival in jeopardy.

Besides responding generously to humanitarian crises, the Church must campaign for international cooperation to reduce our dependence on fossil fuels. Current and future generations depend on decisive action now. As the Oscar-winning film *Parasite* depicted in a powerful parable about one family in Korea, it is the poor who suffer most as the planet heats up. This family's social status is reflected by how they live in a basement beneath ground level. When there is a thunderstorm and a resulting deluge their small home is flooded and awash with sewage, whereas the rich family for whom they work is, by stark contrast, safe at the top of the hill. Working at the food bank and recycling our cardboard, praying for peace, leaving the car on the drive and cycling if we can, and campaigning, are all ways of responding to what God has done for us in Christ. As we grow in Christ's life, we find our hearts and eyes are lifted above our own immediate and local concerns. Sharing in Christ's prayer, we begin to long for the renewal of creation, and for universal justice and peace.

This conversion of life is both a response to and an expression of God's love. Our transformation by God's love is the subject of a virtuous circle: the more we love God, the more we know God, and the more we know God, the more we love God. The writer of *The Cloud of Unknowing*, an anonymous Christian mystical book of the fourteenth century, tells us that the only way to know God is to love God: "By love, he may be touched and embraced, never by thought."[2] In the opening chapter of her book, *Interior Castle*, the sixteenth-century Spanish mystic Teresa of Avila makes the same claim, " . . . love alone, however manifest, leads to union with God . . . ". She underlines the point, "If you would progress a long way along the road, the important thing is not to think much, but to love much. Do then whatever arouses you to love."[3]

Only by loving God can we know the fire of God's love and grow in holiness. In response to a visitor who had reduced Christianity to adhering to a set of rules, Abbot Joseph, one of the Desert Fathers, "rose and lifting his hands against the sky, whereupon his fingers became like ten flaming torches. He then cried, 'If thou wilt, thou shalt be made wholly flame.'"[4] If we desire to know God and to be set ablaze with God's love, we can pray each morning:

> As we rejoice in the gift of this new day, so may the light of your presence, O God, set our hearts on fire with love for you; now and for ever.[5]

The metaphor of fire conveys both the warmth and burning quality of the love of God. God's love is both gracious and demanding. Bracing commands and the gift of grace is the glorious paradox at the heart of our faith. God is experienced as terrible and tender, gentle and purging, just and merciful, yet as only and always love. The white-hot intensity of God's love is experienced in God's judging and purging of our sin. While we must always be wary of making God in our image, we need to be hesitant about losing a sense of God's judgement. Only when we are aware that we need God's mercy are we able to receive it. Only in humility can we come to know and love God more.

Talk of judgement may conjure up pictures of God as a bellicose teacher calling out our name and pointing the finger at us. We reject those types of images because we know that God is kind and merciful. Yet God does hold before us the truth that we were created to fulfil our unique purpose—to become the individuals God has created us to be—and to be full of love. Whereas we know that we are loved just as we are, we are not to be self-satisfied. Knowing God's intention and his ambitious plan to make us more Christlike each day, we seek to become more loving.

As a young boy, whenever I was mean to my sister or had a temper tantrum, the disappointment etched on my parents' faces was enough to prompt me to say sorry and promise to try harder. My love for my mum and dad motivated me to change. In a similar way, our love for God directs our lives and drives our cooperation with God's transforming work in our lives.

Connected with God's judgement is God's wrath which too easily becomes anthropomorphized and confused with ill-tempered individuals and expressions of anger, like shouting, stamping your feet or lashing out, and for that reason is an unpopular, rarely mentioned theological idea, ignored by many, and frequently dismissed as outdated. However, I would contend that we should see it as a reference to the truth that God is implacably opposed to evil. God's wrath is an outworking of God's judgement, and is directed towards those who abuse power and exploit the weak, and relates to his solidarity with those living with injustice. God identifies with the victims of sin and evil, seeking their healing and vindication. Therefore, we can see wrath and compassion combining in God's relentless pursuit of justice: wrath at oppression, and compassion for those oppressed. In our love for God, we must stand with the marginalized and call for a more just world.

We are sustained in this restless pursuit of *shalom*, peace and justice, by the knowledge that the victory has already been won by Christ. The kingdom is coming. We know assuredly that in the end God will triumph. God's glory—the radiant power of God's love—will suffuse the whole world for, as the prophet Habakkuk foresaw: "The earth will be filled with the knowledge of the glory of the Lord, as the waters cover the sea" (Habakkuk 2:14).

Prayer

May the power of your love, Lord Christ,
fiery and sweet,
so absorb our hearts
as to withdraw them from all that is under heaven;
grant that we may be ready
to die for love of your love,
as you died for love of our love. Amen.

Francis of Assisi[6]

CHAPTER 2

Death and resurrection

If for this life only we have hoped in Christ, we are of all people most to be pitied. But in fact Christ has been raised from the dead, the first fruits of those who have died.
1 Corinthians 15:19–20

On being diagnosed with stomach cancer, my mother decided not to have any treatment. Following a conversation with the oncologist, she concluded that though a course of chemotherapy might prolong her life for a few weeks, she would have to endure nausea and fatigue, and her quality of life would be excessively impaired. In this courageous decision, she had accepted her mortality. She had begun to prepare to die.

Three months or so later, her life ended in a hospice with her husband, daughter and son by her bedside. As her breath began to falter and fade, my sister, a nurse, moistened her parched lips, adjusted her pillow and tried to keep her comfortable. My dad looked at her gaunt face; he was attentive, yet tired and agonized by grief. When her breathing finally stopped, I said prayers of thanksgiving and commendation, as my dad and sister wept quietly beside me.

Twenty years later I realize, even more clearly than at the time, that I saw the strength of my mum's faith most vividly as she faced her mortality and neared the end of her life. I had witnessed a holy death.

Confidence in the face of death

My mother's courage in facing death head-on was informed by a calculation of what was in her best interests but was inspired by her faith in God. Over the weeks from diagnosis to death, she remained largely unperturbed by her physical deterioration—weightloss and listlessness—and some bouts of discomfort. She slowly withdrew from her circle of friends, declining visits. In the last few weeks, apart from the staff at the hospice, she only saw me, my dad and my sister. As her outer world shrank, her inner life seemed to strengthen. Physically diminished and less engaged with the wider world, she was focusing her remaining energy on her immediate family, and turning her attention to God. She believed that Christ is risen, and death is vanquished, and eternity with God beyond death awaited her. This confidence in God was reflected in the inscription on her headstone, "With Christ which is far better" (Philippians 1:23, NKJV).

Paradoxically, Christ defeats death by dying. By his death—his voluntary self-offering—Christ conquers death. The language associated with victory over death is based on the idea that death is not simply the point when life ends but rather an enemy to be fought. In the Christian tradition, death is conceived as humanity's foe, with whom we are locked in mortal combat. John Diamond, the *Times* journalist, who chronicled his experience of throat cancer from diagnosis to death in the Saturday magazine, spoke of seeing a personification of death as he realized that his condition could be terminal. In one piece, he described a shadowy, slightly embarrassed figure, lurking behind the consultant, clutching a scythe.[7] This reference is to the mythological character, the Grim Reaper, usually pictured as a human skeleton covered by a shroud, ready to reap the living. For all of us, the prospect of dying lies before us. While thoughts of our mortality become more frequent as we grow older, we know, whatever our age, that death is coming. We know too that Jesus has already confronted death in a decisive and final battle, and won.

Our anxiety about death is generally unacknowledged but is, in fact, revealed by our determined attempts not to talk about it. In most circles, death is a taboo subject in conversation and a reality from which we shy away. Few of us have seen a corpse before one of our parents dies. Our public rituals surrounding death have been largely abandoned: gone are the days when everyone stopped walking and paid their respects when a hearse passed, and most drivers no longer give way to a funeral cortège.

Most funeral services happen in crematoria, out of town, and hidden away. Our muted emotions at funerals led an observer from a nation where wailing and weeping is the norm to comment that we mourn as though no one has died. There is also an increasing emphasis at funerals on celebrating the life rather than mourning the death. We cannot, though, evade our sense of loss. In truth, the more we celebrate the life, the stronger our awareness of what we have lost. Loss and celebration are intrinsically bound together; even our treasured memories of the deceased make us conscious of their absence. To those with insight, these attempts to conceal our anxiety about dying and death do the opposite: they expose it.

Another feature of our culture's denial of death is our obsession with youth. Oscar Wilde famously said, "Youth is wasted on the young." Those who are older tend to envy the young their energy and vitality. Not surprisingly, therefore, as we age, we want to appear younger than we are. We usually reserve the label "old" for people at least ten years older than ourselves. The cosmetic industry fosters this fear of looking our age to sell us the delusion that we can turn the clock back, or at least stop it for a while. Facelifts can remove some wrinkles and Botox can stretch the skin but the fear of ageing still lingers. "Growing old" does bring its losses and accompanying challenges. As someone said to me, "It is not for the faint-hearted", but we need not be afraid of the latter stages of our life. It is possible to age gracefully and to face death calmly, even confidently.

We see in the Gospels that Jesus foresees his death. He knowingly heads towards Jerusalem for the final time but is not cowed by what awaits him there. On his arrival in the city, packed with pilgrims there for the Passover, he claims through two symbolic acts that he is the Messiah. Both are bound to outrage the religious authorities and trouble the politicians: his triumphal entry into Jerusalem and his dressing down of the money changers in the temple. As he enters Jerusalem on a donkey in dramatic fulfilment of an Old Testament prophecy about a future king, the crowds cheer and hail him as the "one who comes in the name of the Lord". Those in power see him as a threat and plot his downfall

(Matthew 21:1–13). Following his condemnation of the corrupt practices in the temple, they decide that Jesus must die. On his journey towards Jerusalem, we can say that there is already a gun against his head. After his protest in the temple, the trigger is cocked.

When we ask, "Why did Jesus die?" we can answer by referring to the way he confronted those in power, the political explanation. Alternatively, we can give the theological response that in the cross, God confronts humanity's twin enemies, sin and death, and defeats them. Through his death, Christ experiences our mortality and embraces death. His corpse is taken down from the cross and placed in a tomb. His lifeless body seems to reveal Jesus as yet another false messiah. All his talk of God's kingdom has come to nothing and he has endured a bloody, undignified death. Yet, this is not the end because Jesus once more confounds expectations.

At the centre of the life of this charismatic healer and teacher from Galilee is the deeper reality of an intimate relationship with God the Father. As the Son of God, Christ shares God's eternal life: there is no way, therefore, that he can remain dead. By his resurrection, Christ enters his risen life, and sets us free from death's grip. Since we participate in his eternal life here and now, we are liberated from our fear at death's relentless approach.

This is everlasting life because it is God's life, but we experience this new life with God in the present. Our participation in eternal life is a sharing in the death and resurrection of Christ. Living in Christ, we know his death—we die—and his resurrection—we rise—in the events, relationships, and circumstances of our day-to-day lives. Sharing in his dying and rising in life is a preparation for experiencing his dying and rising in our physical death.

In Christ, we can stand resolute as we grieve for someone or for our own death, knowing that death leads to resurrection. We meet dying and death on the sure ground of Christ's resurrection and look forward to a bodily resurrection, an embodied life in God's kingdom. John Donne's poem "Death be not proud" expresses this robust confidence that death is defeated, and our mortality is a gateway into eternity with God:

> Death, be not proud, though some have called thee
> Mighty and dreadful, for thou art not so;
> For those whom thou think'st thou dost overthrow
> Die not, poor Death, nor yet canst thou kill me.
> From rest and sleep, which but thy pictures be,
> Much pleasure; then from thee much more must flow,
> And soonest our best men with thee do go,
> Rest of their bones, and soul's delivery.
> Thou art slave to fate, chance, kings, and desperate men,
> And dost with poison, war, and sickness dwell,
> And poppy or charms can make us sleep as well
> And better than thy stroke; why swell'st thou then?
> One short sleep past, we wake eternally
> And death shall be no more; Death, thou shalt die.[8]

Dying and rising in Christ

In the three synoptic Gospels—Matthew, Mark and Luke—this link between following Jesus and knowing his death is expressed in the call to "take up your cross". Carrying our crosses and following Christ, we discover that death is not just the event that marks the end of our lives but a daily reality (Luke 9:23). We discover each day that our discipleship is characterized by self-giving, sacrificial love. In every step we take towards Christ, we die to self, and live to God (Colossians 3:3). As we walk the way of the cross, Christ, who is always ahead of us beckoning us forwards, is also beside us to give us the strength we need when we falter and lose courage. We need to remember too that, in many parts of the world, Christians are still martyred for their faith. In those places, the summons to "take up your cross daily" has a stronger resonance with Jesus' walk to Golgotha and his crucifixion.

As we emulate Jesus by laying down our lives for God and others, we know his death and resurrection. In loving those around us whatever the cost, we are bound to make sacrifices. These acts of self-giving love can be seen as a series of "little deaths". By each "little death" we grow in love and get ready step by step to face our physical death. This is what it means to walk the way of the cross. When we go on visiting our friend in the nursing home who can no longer remember our name and will have forgotten that we have been as soon as we have left, we know that love and loss are often woven together in life. We experience the generous love of the cross. When we support a friend, who is battling with addiction, and see their self-esteem plummet and their life ebb away, we embrace the pain of the cross. Even when we do something apparently trivial because of love, such as tidying the kitchen, even though it is not our turn, we embrace the cross. When we obey God's summons to us to move to a new house and change jobs, even though we are settled and fulfilled, we die to our selfishness and choose the cross. Any action, however great or small, done in obedience to God's call to grow in love, is to know Christ's death. In this "dying of discipleship", we discover that the beauty of love arises out of the sacrifices we make.

The legend of the thorn bird speaks of how selfless, costly acts of love for others are supremely beautiful. It is about a bird which sings just once in its life, more sweetly than any other creature on the face of the earth, bringing great joy to those who hear its song. From the moment it leaves the nest it searches for a thorn tree, and does not rest until it has found one, longing to sing for the whole world. Then, singing among the savage branches, it impales itself upon the longest, sharpest spine. And, dying, it rises above its own agony to out-carol the lark and the nightingale —all activity elsewhere ceases, as everyone stops, still and attentive, to listen.

Our physical death is, of course, the ultimate test of our discipleship: the decisive moment when we see how attached our hearts are to this world, and discover how strong is our longing for yet greater intimacy with God in heaven. Letting go of life and those we love is far from easy. Saying "farewell" to those who we have loved so much for so long can be heartbreaking and gut-wrenching. We can be confident, though, that as we trust God, even in the grief of our own dying, we bear witness to God's strength in human frailty and weakness (2 Corinthians 12:9).

Baptized into Christ's death

We can sing and read about the cross. We can study the various theories explaining what Christ's death achieves for us. This can all be helpful and does give us valuable insights into the significance of the cross. Yet this is all from the perspective of an observer, someone trying to understand this event from afar. As Christians, though, we are not merely spectators, we are participants, and the only way truly to understand Christ's death, truly, is to share in it. We believe as Christians that we are not lookers-on at Calvary; we are one with Christ in his dying and death. Being in Christ, we discover that his experience of crucifixion is ours. We are nailed to those wooden beams too: we are crucified with Christ. Each of us can say with Paul, "I have been crucified with Christ" (Galatians 2:19).

In our baptism, we are plunged into his death, and we live out our baptism by dying daily. Paul explains that through our baptism, we share in Christ's death. We are thereby dead to the power of sin (Romans 6:1–4). Whereas the question "Have you been baptized?" is crucially important, the pressing one is "Are you baptized?" Baptism is much more than a past event; it is a lived reality. We can see the photographs, frame the certificate, hear or tell the stories about the "big day". That we have been baptized matters. Its impact, however, is embraced or negated in the choices we make now and in the priorities that shape our lives. If we decide to serve, choose to love whoever we meet, seek to love God in all things, then we know the transforming power of Christ's death.

This kind of knowledge cannot be gleaned from a book or be taught in a classroom. It is like becoming a swimmer: we can wave our arms around on the side of the pool, imitating front crawl and breaststroke, but at some point, we are going to have to get in the pool and begin trying to swim. Likewise, we can watch others cycling on the roads around us. We can see Chris Froome win the Tour de France on the small screen, and we can buy a state-of-the-art bike, stand it carefully in the garage and imagine ourselves shooting up a nearby hill effortlessly, but if we want to learn to ride, we have no choice but to get on the saddle and start pedalling. Similarly, we can only grasp the meaning of Christ's death by participation, by experiencing it and by living it.

Jesus teaches his disciples that they will not only see him die but will share in his death. In John's Gospel, Peter tells Jesus, "I will lay down my life for you" (John 13:37). Jesus knows that Peter's claim is premature, more bravado than bravery. He is not ready to die for Jesus, not yet prepared to share in his death, and Jesus foretells Peter's denial. He foresees that before the cock crows, Peter will refute that he knows Jesus three times. After he is risen, Jesus reinstates Peter as a disciple when he asks him three times, "Do you love me?" Peter replies to each question with increasing vehemence, "You know that I love you." Peter had come to understand that the fundamental choice of Christian discipleship is denial or death, and now does not baulk at Jesus' prophecy that he will be martyred, and responds obediently to Jesus' renewed summons to "follow me" (John 21:15–19).

To follow Christ is to reject a life independent of God, the source of life that can only lead to isolation and alienation from God, ourselves, and, ultimately, from others. In serving Christ and shouldering our cross, we have a life centred on Christ and his other disciples. By living for Christ, we become more who we were created to be and discover that "to serve Christ is perfect freedom".[9]

In Mark 10, James and John, two of Jesus' disciples, ask for preferment when Christ becomes king. They want influential and important positions in Christ's kingly court, but their request is based on a false assumption, namely that Jesus is to lead a rebellion to usurp the Roman authorities and install himself as king. Their self-promotion reveals their ambition, their own desire for prestige and power, and that they misunderstand his messiahship. Their self-interest and competitive calculations are unmasked as Jesus challenges both their understanding of his messiahship, and what it means to follow him, in his promise that they will share in his death: "The cup that I drink you will drink; and with the baptism with which I am baptized, you will be baptized" (Mark 10:39). Baptism here is a metaphor for death, and Jesus tells these two disciples that like every one of his followers, they will know his death in their lives. Their daily dying to self will find its fullest expression when they are asked, like Peter, to make the ultimate sacrifice and be martyrs for the Christ they follow. Being a disciple of Christ is going where he leads and imitating the pattern of his life, and that means that we love sacrificially, and are prepared to die for our faith.

Christ emptied himself and humbled himself, to live in obedience to God and to die on the cross (Philippians 2:5–11). Frank Sinatra's famous song "My Way" is the antithesis of this attitude of humble obedience: "I did it my way . . . I did what I had to do . . . I planned each chartered course, each careful step along the byway . . . I did it my way." This song is a fanfare for the rugged individual and an anthem to self-determination. In stark contrast, Christians give up their own agenda and follow Christ, seeking to live according to "Christ's Way".

Any attempts to live independently of others and God are folly and are futile. The myth of the self-made individual is fundamentally a lie because our lives are inextricably interconnected with others. We are embedded in a network of formative relationships with our family and friends. We are united in one nation and one world through our social, political and economic structures. We depend upon others for the food on our plate, and we become who we are through the people who shape us. Any claim to self-sufficiency mocks reality and underplays the loving relationships that are central to human flourishing. As Christians, we are thankful for our dependence on God, the source of life and love, and our interdependence. We delight in the mutuality of love, and the giving and receiving of each other's gifts.

In our churches, we set our hearts on serving God and each other, and to learning what it means to belong to a community. Each church is a "school for discipleship", a community in which we are to grow in love and service. In our conversations before and after services, in small groups for prayer and Bible study, in our more formal meetings too, we learn to sense each other's needs and value each other's gifts. When we give and receive within the church's life, we make the most of our mutual dependence, and nourish our life together. "This week, I need you to encourage me, and next week, when you ask me to support you, I'll be there for you." This reciprocal interdependence characterizes our churches at their best. Through the giving and receiving of love, this holy exchange, we die to our own self-centredness and are joined in love. By allowing someone to serve us, we acknowledge our vulnerability, effectively saying to them, "I need you." Only through this openness to one another can we learn to love each other, and witness to and share God's generous love with the world.

The continual call to repentance

To die to selfishness, we need repeatedly to hear and heed the call to repentance. None of us can contend that we obey fully the two great commandments to love God and our neighbour as ourselves (Mark 12:28–34). When we know that we have fallen short on an occasion or in a relationship, we are not to find excuses or explanations or bewail how we have been treated or wish our circumstances were different; we need, instead, to put our trust in God simply and lovingly, and acknowledge our lack of love.

I know that when I have made a mistake or not done what I should have done, my first reaction can be defensive. I rattle off a stream of reasons why I was not at my best. These valiant attempts to put me in a better light do not fool the listeners, and certainly leave God unimpressed.

When I attended a speed awareness course, the leaders stated at the beginning of the first session that they did not need to know our excuses. They had heard them all before, and they did not want to waste everyone's time. I had been ready with mine: "I was in Wales and didn't know the roads, which were clear, and I was in a hurry." I am sure that I was not the only one with an explanation lined up. We would all have aimed to soften our offence with stories of why we were speeding and to assure everyone that we were good drivers, and had nothing to learn.

Rather than look for excuses or to pass the blame, Jesus tells us to acknowledge our mistakes straightforwardly, saying, for example, "I am in the wrong. I am sorry." This simple admission is so easy to say, unless it is you that has to take responsibility for your actions or inaction, and own up. Our pride protests. Yet, Jesus urges us to be humble in his repeated refrain: "All who exalt themselves will be humbled, and those who humble themselves will be exalted" (Luke 14:11; 18:14). We need to learn to say "sorry" simply, without any condition, such as "If I have hurt you" or "If I got that wrong", and to forgive in a similarly direct manner. This straightforward approach to confession and forgiveness is based on the awareness of two fundamental Christian truths that we are all fallible and God is merciful.

Sometimes we can be wrongly accused, and despite our best efforts find our reputation has been damaged. We can, in these situations, find some consolation in remembering that Christ was misunderstood and rejected. When we lose face or incur disapproval unfairly, we have an opportunity to identify consciously with Christ in his suffering and sorrow.

In his letter to the persecuted church in Rome, where many were being martyred for their faith in Christ, Paul encouraged the Christians there to persevere, telling them, "Suffering produces endurance, and endurance produces character, and character produces hope, and hope does not disappoint us, because God's love has been poured into our hearts through the Holy Spirit that has been given to us" (Romans 5:3–5). By sharing in Christ's death, we experience Christ's resurrection, and the joy and love of the Holy Spirit. This leads to our growth in love for God and for others.

When life is hard . . .

When life is hard, we can offer our struggles to God, who gives us the courage we need. By accepting our present circumstances, we trust whatever is happening is within God's providence. Putting our faith anew in God, we find fresh strength. The truth is that whatever we face, we are never beyond the scope of God to help us. Rather than grumble or blame others, we deliberately place our lives once more in God's hands, and open ourselves to God's peace that is beyond our understanding but within our experience. By persevering in faith, we are taken deeper into Christ and know that God does not test us beyond our power to endure: God is faithful, and we can rest in his love (1 Corinthians 10:13).

While we do what we can to improve our life and the lives of those around us, we learn to accept what we cannot change, and, thereby, foster a basic calmness. The serenity prayer denotes that we need wisdom to discern when we are to be passive, surrendered to God in our current circumstances, and when we need to be active, seeking to make life better: "God grant me the serenity to accept the things that I cannot change, courage to change the things that I can, and wisdom to know the difference."[10]

By cultivating a basic contentment with life each day, however it pans out, we prepare for those times when the landscape of our lives is rugged and bleak. Even when the way ahead looks pretty barren, we can experience God's abiding peace. As we set our minds to endure, and press on, trusting in God, we can learn to pray as Catherine of Siena, a mystic and author in the fourteenth century, did, "Lord, as you will, and how you will, for as long as you will."

Sometimes, though, we are bound to feel like giving up. The burden we are carrying seems too heavy; we simply cannot cope with another day, another hour, of life as it is. In the vulnerability of feeling that we can no longer carry on—when we feel worn out—we are particularly open to the tender love of God. In the famous poem *Footprints*, there are two sets of footprints in the sand, God's and the author's, denoting that at each step God has been with her, a steady and reliable companion. Yet, looking over her entire life, she notices that during her times of grief and suffering there was only one set of footprints. Puzzled that God seemed to have deserted her when she needed God the most, she asks God pointedly for an explanation. God replies, "My daughter, my precious child, I love you and will never leave you. During your times of trial and suffering, when you see only one set of footprints, it was then that I carried you." When we can no longer walk, God picks us up in his arms and carries us. When it all seems just too much, and we feel that we have nothing further to give, we can let go and fall into God's loving embrace. The title of one of Corrie ten Boom's books—she helped many Jewish families escape the Nazis in Holland in the Second World War—conveys how we are to stop striving and instead are to fall into the arms of God: *Don't Wrestle, Just Nestle*. Whilst perhaps a little corny, this maxim does convey that sense of ceasing to struggle and simply resting in God. Therefore, in our journey through life, when we feel that we cannot go on, we are to call on the name of Jesus, who will come with the Father and the Holy Spirit and enfold us in love.

Death, resurrection, ascension, and the gift of the Spirit

In the Eucharist, we are drawn into the death and resurrection of Christ—the Paschal Mystery—and ascend with Christ to the Father. This one movement takes us into heaven where we are renewed in the power of the Holy Spirit. Entering into heaven, we realize the mystical reality of our dual citizenship: we are residents of the earth where we live out our discipleship but also citizens of heaven. The writer of the letter to the Colossians urges us, "Set your minds on things that are above, not on things that are on earth, for you have died, and your life is hidden with Christ in God" (Colossians 3:2–3).

To celebrate and live out the Eucharist—always, whatever life brings, giving thanks to God the Father through Christ—is to share in the dying and rising of Christ. As death and resurrection mark the rhythm of our lives we participate too in Christ's ascension and are renewed by the Holy Spirit. Centred on the crucified and Risen Christ and knowing the peace and joy of the Holy Spirit, we witness to God's light and truth.

In the great nineteenth-century Russian author Fyodor Dostoevsky's classic book *The Idiot*, one of the characters, Prince Myschkin, reports how a young mother exemplified the full life that is the theme of the book. He tells of how he saw her cross herself when her baby smiled for the first time. On asking her why she had made the sign of her faith, she explained that her delight in her child's happiness had reminded her of God's joy when we pray, "God has just such gladness every time God sees from heaven that a sinner is praying to him with all his heart as a mother when she sees the first smile on a baby's face."[11] Through her simple expression of faith, Prince Myschkin sees the essence of Christianity, because this mother is living in the light of God's truth. In seeing the joy she has discovered in Christ, he is disconcerted. His disbelief is undermined, and he becomes more open to God (Romans 14:17).

Our daily discipleship and witness to our faith in the world are vital to our effective participation in the Eucharist. Our lives are to be integrated: what we know in the Eucharist, we live, and what we live, we offer in the Eucharist. With and in Christ, we are shown how to die that we may rise, ascend to the Father, and receive the outpoured Holy Spirit anew. This life-giving dynamic is at the heart of the Eucharist and is the truth from which flows our discipleship.

Prayer

Thanks be to thee, our Lord Jesus Christ, for all the benefits which thou hast won for us, for the pains and insults which thou hast borne for us. O most merciful Redeemer, Friend, and Brother, may we know thee more clearly, love thee more dearly, and follow thee more nearly, day by day. Amen.

Richard of Chichester[12]

CHAPTER 3

Do this in remembrance of me

Unleavened bread shall be eaten for seven days; no leavened bread shall be seen in your possession, and no leaven shall be seen among you in all your territory. You shall tell your child on that day, "It is because of what the Lord did for me when I came out of Egypt."

Exodus 13:7–8

On the Tomlinson family summer holidays, we always reminisce over previous ones at some point, rating locations and recalling highlights. Some years, we have tried to link each holiday with its corresponding year, which is not an easy task; muddling up the order, though, is part of the fun. We often seek to rank them in terms of how much we enjoyed each one but never reach entire agreement. Some of my favourite memories include: walking to Corfe Castle along the ridge from Swanage on a sunny morning and spotting a deer; the dinner at a restaurant on the walls of the old city in Dubrovnik overlooking the harbour; eating pizza on the beach at Argelès-sur-Mer in the South of France on a balmy evening; and the walk up and the view from the top of Pen y Fan in the Brecon Beacons. Recounting and reliving these special times remind us of our shared narrative as a family, our ongoing journey through life together. Our holidays are enriched by these conversations, often over dinner, al fresco if the weather allows; and by remembering the past, we deepen the delight we have in each other's company and the love between us in the present.

You are my witnesses

The call to remember the Last Supper is based on the eye-witness record of those first disciples who were there when Jesus took the loaf of bread and the cup, and told them, "Do this in remembrance of me" (1 Corinthians 11:23–6). The Eucharist is a faithful response to this command; the liturgy of the service is an expanded remembrance of Jesus. We recall who he is in relation to God the Father and the Holy Spirit, what he taught and what he accomplished for us. We celebrate how he is present with us to save us and transform our lives now. We look forward to when we will see Jesus face to face at the End, when the kingdom comes and earth and heaven are one.

In this act of collective remembrance, we are mindful of how Jesus taught that the two great commandments to love God and neighbour are the summary of the laws and prophetic sayings of the Old Testament. For Jesus, this dual mandate is the heart of Scripture's instruction on how to live the good life, the godly life:

> When the Pharisees heard that he had silenced the Sadducees, they gathered together, and one of them, a lawyer, asked him a question to test him. "Teacher, which commandment in the law is the greatest?" He said to him, "'You shall love the Lord your God with all your heart, and with all your soul, and with all your mind.' This is the greatest and first commandment. And a second is like it: 'You shall love your neighbour as yourself.' On these two commandments hang all the law and the prophets."
>
> *Matthew 22:34–40*

In the Eucharist, we are reminded of this imperative to love God and our neighbour and affirm that we are God's people subject to God's commands. We recall too that God has forgiven us and set us free to learn to love as Jesus loves.

By listening to and entering into the Gospel accounts of Jesus' healing and storytelling, of his grace and his judgement, of his forgiveness and his challenge to love generously, we share the experience of his first followers. In this encounter with Jesus and his companions through the Gospels, we learn to express his words and actions in the place where we live today and become his witnesses.

Freddie Mercury and Elton John have been depicted in biopic films on the big screen. On television, we have seen the Queen portrayed in the series entitled *The Crown*. These skilled performances are more than impersonations. Rather the actor must understand their character from the inside, to see how they had been shaped by their back story, and so grasp what makes them tick, what moves and motivates them. Like these actors, we must immerse ourselves in Jesus' story. Seeing how he relates to friend, stranger and enemy, we learn how to love everyone we meet. When we see how many were captivated by this charismatic, itinerant, story-telling wonder-worker, we are drawn closer to him. Finding how many were not sure what to make of him, we know that there is always more to learn about him. Noticing how he excited the crowds and delighted those who were marginalized, we absorb and share the infectious generosity he generated around him. When we realize again that some followed him yet many did not, and others plotted to have him killed, we know that we have to go on choosing to follow him, and what the cost of discipleship is. We return repeatedly to the Gospels to imbibe the life of Jesus, like a thirsty gazelle to its water hole. Again, and again, we immerse ourselves in these narratives and emerge each time better able to face the present challenges of following Christ. Our shared task is to translate our familiarity with Jesus in the Gospels into a common life that is energized by his life amongst us today. Responding to his presence with us, we are to let him shape our lives and lead us into the future.

As we become more attuned to the rhythms of Christ's life with us, our discipleship becomes less deliberate and more habitual. We become accustomed to his gentle grace and learn to relate to each other in love. His patient, attentive focus is reflected in our conversations with others. Our discipleship moves from a self-conscious mimicking towards a self-forgetful emulating of the Christ we follow. Gradually, his life is lived through us.

Being Christ's representatives today in a sometimes hostile and often seemingly disinterested world can be daunting. Yet we are to remain confident that the Holy Spirit enables us to share Christ's life with the world. We must remember Jesus' promise: "When the Holy Spirit comes, you will be my witnesses" (Acts 1:8). Besides telling others about Jesus, we are to present him in all we do, in our speaking and listening, in our relating and loving, in every aspect of our lives (2 Corinthians 5:20). This is a responsibility that demands prayerful thought and wisdom but is also a privilege and a joy.

Minding the gap between "then and there" and "here and now"

On the evening before my ordination to the diaconate, the Bishop of Guildford, the Rt Revd Michael Adie, spoke to all those to be ordained the following morning. He urged us to be first and foremost disciples of Jesus, and counselled us that only by making this our top priority would our ministries bear lasting fruit. He told us that as we work out what it means to follow Jesus now, we must first soak ourselves in the New Testament, and especially the Gospels, but we must then pay attention to the changed context: life in modern Britain is very different from life in first-century Galilee. He underlined this point with a visual image that has stayed with me ever since. Whenever we interpret the Scriptures and apply them to our lives, we are to call to mind the tannoy announcement when an underground train pulls into a London station. When the doors begin to open and before those on the platform begin to file on to the train, we hear the warning, "Mind the gap. Mind the gap." Through this memorable illustration, he reminded us to be aware of the gap between the world of the New Testament and our own context in our prayerful task of witnessing to Jesus today.

When we ask, "What would Jesus do?", we often cannot simply look for a parallel case in the Gospels and do exactly now what Jesus did then. To take one subject, we do not seek to dress like we imagine Jesus did—sandals and long white robe—or travel solely as Jesus did—on foot or by donkey. There is no reason to think that Jesus would have been averse to taking a car, riding a bike or going on the bus. However, we could argue from Jesus' love of the Father and the Father's world, and with the urgent need to reduce fuel emissions, that when opportunity allows, riding our bikes or walking are preferable to the bus, and taking the car is the worst of those options.

Karl Barth, a famous German theologian in the twentieth century, said about the preaching task, "Take your Bible and take a newspaper; read both. But interpret newspapers from the Bible."[13] What is true for those preparing sermons is true for every facet of our discipleship: we are to look at our present reality and the Gospels together, but remember to read our time through the Gospels because they are our starting point. When we encounter issues that Jesus did not face, such as the morality of the arms trade, or when we know much more about a subject now than then, for instance, gender, sexuality, disease, and mental health, prayerful thought and reasoned argument are required. Whatever we are considering, the goal remains the same: our resulting actions must be true to Jesus as we see him in the Gospels and know him in our present context. To realize this goal, we need to attend to Jesus, in the Gospels and in our midst, looking to the Holy Spirit to guide us.

Remembrance is participation

In the Old Testament, we see how important it is for God's people to celebrate their history. Their annual feasts take them back to the formative events that forged and still define their identity, and provide continuity down the centuries. Many take them back to the Exodus, their liberation from tyranny and bondage, and their journey to the Promised Land. For instance, they are told to recall the Passover each year for ever. "This day shall be a day of remembrance for you. You shall celebrate it as a festival to the Lord; throughout your generations you shall observe it as a perpetual ordinance" (Exodus 12:14). As each generation celebrates the Passover, the unity of God's people is renewed and defines those gathered as "the people God rescued from Egypt".

The Passover meal commemorates God's deliverance of God's people from oppression in Egypt. On the day of their escape, they slaughtered lambs and daubed the door frames of their houses with the lamb's blood. This bloody marker set them apart on this fateful night. When the first-born Egyptian children were struck dead, the "destroyer" passed over the homes of the Israelites (Exodus 12). In reaction to this catastrophic event and his nation's overwhelming grief, Pharaoh finally relents, and tells Moses and Aaron, Israel's leaders, that he will submit to their repeated plea, made on behalf of God: "Let my people go." The Israelites were ready and left swiftly that night.

Through the festival of the Passover, each succeeding generation identifies with those who fled from Egypt. Those who keep the feast go back to Egypt and experience God's rescue for themselves. By their remembrance, they are more than spectators, gazing into the past from a distant time; they become participants in history. They enter into the Exodus, the foundational event for God's people, so fully, that they can say for themselves, "We were set free from bondage in Egypt." The Passover is the memorial whereby each succeeding generation of God's people is united with those who packed up and fled, with those who panicked at the Red Sea but ended up trudging through the mud to the other side, with those who hailed their deliverance on the shore and then tramped through the wilderness, and with all those countless people who have celebrated the Passover over the centuries: they are all one.

In the New Testament, the death of Christ is interpreted through the lens of the Passover. Parallels are drawn between the liberation Christ wins from sin and death and the freedom from oppression secured in the Exodus. Christ is described as the Passover lamb who has been sacrificed, and the redemption won by Christ as a new Exodus. Like the function of the Passover in the life of the nation, the Eucharist is a setting forth of the foundational event of the Church: Christ's death and resurrection, the Paschal Mystery.

The Exodus formed God's people and put them under obligation to God. As God had rescued them, they were to live in the light of this generous act. In response to God's grace, they are to live distinctively, by obeying the Ten Commandments that begin, tellingly, "I am the Lord your God, who brought you out of the land of Egypt, out of the house of slavery; you shall have no other gods before me" (Exodus 20:2–3). In the New Testament, God's people are defined as those who know Christ's death and centre their life together on the Risen Christ. The Eucharist is a proclamation of Christ's death and a celebration of Christ's risen life:

it is the Church's constitutive event. The Church's identity is renewed in the Eucharist.

In the Eucharist, as we remember the Last Supper, we find ourselves seated at the table and can look around at those gathered with Jesus, Judas, John, Peter and all the other disciples. Then we leave the upper room, and go to Golgotha, moving from the intimacy of sharing bread and wine with Jesus to the horror of his body racked with pain on the cross. We enter into the Passion of Christ.

By reliving Christ's Passion, we commemorate this formative event for the Church. We re-enact Jesus' taking, blessing, and sharing of the bread and the wine at his last meal with his friends. We recall his crucifixion. Praying through these events in the Eucharistic Prayer is described as an act of "remembrance" or making "the memorial" of his death. In revisiting and inhabiting these events, we behold his Passion in God's presence.

It may seem that the only way we can be at the cross is to engage in time travel and to journey to Jerusalem. However, the present reality of the cross in the Eucharist and our everyday lives is not the result of a feat of our imaginations but is grounded in the presence of Christ with us. In the incarnation, the eternal Son becomes flesh and blood like you and me, and eternity enters into time (John 1:14). That means that what happens in Jesus' earthly life has an eternal dimension. We can consider this truth in another way: as Jesus is fully human and fully God, his life, every day and each event, is both transient in time and eternal. Thereby, the cross is both a past event in history, and at the same time an eternal event with eternal significance, and so a present event in which we can participate.

We are drawn deeper into Christ's self-offering expressed definitively on the cross, not by flight of fancy or a monumental effort of will, but by the Holy Spirit. In God's eternal now, we share in Christ's self-offering on the cross and are taken deeper into the life of God. When we celebrate the Eucharist, the Holy Spirit brings together our worship and Christ's self-offering to God on the cross, making them one offering to God. The Eucharistic Prayer B in *Common Worship* culminates with this great sense of those gathered being offered to the Father in Christ in the Holy Spirit:

> Send the Holy Spirit on your people
> and gather into one in your kingdom
> all who share this one bread and one cup,
> so that we, in the company of all the saints,
> may praise and glorify you for ever,
> through Jesus Christ our Lord;
>
> by whom, and with whom, and in whom,
> in the unity of the Holy Spirit,
> all honour and glory be yours, almighty Father,
> for ever and ever. Amen.[14]

In our act of corporate remembrance, the linear course of time is transcended, and we stand before the cross. By the power of the Holy Spirit, we participate in Christ's Passion, not just as spectators, watching Christ suffer and die, but as those drawn into Christ's life, participants in his death and resurrection. This mystical experience reflects the prior truth that we have already been included in Christ's self-offering on the cross. Through his humanity, Christ offers the whole of humanity, each human being throughout time, to the Father. As Christ's life of self-offering is consummated in his death, we are included in Christ's sacrifice, integral to what Christ gives to the Father. Therefore, each day, we can know the truth that we have already been offered to God in Christ's death. At the end of our lives, knowing that we have already been commended to God in his death, we can pray confidently Jesus' final words as he surrenders his life to the Father, "Father, into your hands I commend my spirit" (Luke 23:46).

Being with Jesus

Those who were with Jesus—who saw him, touched him and heard him—are the credible witnesses who validate our remembrance of Christ in the Eucharist. It is their account, and particularly their record of his death and resurrection, which has enabled successive generations to enact the memorial of Christ's life. That is why the Church is called "apostolic": it is founded on the collective memory of those first followers of Jesus Christ. They show us how an established relationship with him is transformative because their distinguishing characteristic was that they had "been with Jesus" (Acts 4:13). They were witnesses to the resurrection because they had eaten and drunk with him after he rose from the dead (Acts 10:40–1). After Jesus returned to the Father, they continued to eat and drink with the Risen Christ in the power of the Holy Spirit in the Eucharist. Their ongoing witness was still to the Christ in their midst. Their eschatological role—their place in God's kingdom—is linked to their being Jesus' disciples, for he said to them, "Truly I tell you, at the renewal of all things, when the Son of Man is seated on the throne of his glory, you who have followed me will also sit on twelve thrones, judging the twelves tribes of Israel" (Matthew 19:28).

In the Eucharist, we celebrate the memorial of our redemption, our deliverance from sin and death by God in Christ on the cross. Having encountered Christ and known the redeeming work of God, we go out to continue his reconciling ministry to an increasingly fractured and fragmented world. We go to proclaim who Jesus is, to make known what he has done, and to share what he is doing, for the Christ we remember is with us.

Prayer

> O Father, give the spirit power to climb to the fountain of all light, and be purified. Break through the mists of earth, the weight of the clod. Shine forth in splendour, thou art calm weather and a quiet resting place for faithful souls. To see thee is the end and the beginning. Thou carriest us, and thou dost go before us. Thou art the journey and the journey's end.
>
> *Boethius*[15]

CHAPTER 4

The Holy Spirit

Be filled with the Spirit.

Ephesians 5:18

Because of his rotund build and kind-hearted personality, the Scout District Commissioner, Fred, was known affectionately as the Fat Controller, after the manager of the North Western Railway in the Thomas the Tank Engine series, who is a father figure to his engines. During one St George's Day parade service which I was leading, a cub scout came to the front to do a reading. As I handed him the microphone, I could see that he was nervous and offered him a reassuring smile. He turned to face the congregation of over three hundred people and, his voice quavering, he began. He stumbled over the first few words and then stopped. Fred hurried to join him at the front and, speaking softly, told him to take a breath and start again, and not to worry. He stood beside him as the boy inhaled deeply and began again. At first, he was hesitant, but soon he was reading fluently. As his confidence returned, his clear voice filled the church. The District Commissioner's presence by his side had given him strength, enabling him to find his voice and releasing him to do his best.

Fred's role in this story illustrates one of the alternative titles for the Holy Spirit, the "Paraclete", which means "one called alongside" to help. As the cub scout was bolstered to read as well as he could by the presence of the District Commissioner beside him, the Holy Spirit is with us to help us to be disciples, to release us from all that holds us back. We are given the Holy Spirit to help us to pray, to worship, and to love God in every aspect of our lives.

The gift of the Holy Spirit

We can only respond to God's call to deepen our discipleship if our dependence on the Holy Spirit grows. Since discipleship and dependence on God go hand in hand, we need to be increasingly filled with the Holy Spirit. The command, "Be filled with the Spirit", assumes that a disciple is like a receptacle and the Spirit like a liquid (Ephesians 5:18). The Father who is pouring out the Spirit longs to fill the container to the brim; he desires that we be full of the Spirit. It is only our incapacity to receive the Spirit that determines how full we are, not any reluctance on God's part to fill us.

In Luke's Gospel, Jesus makes this clear in one of his "how much more" parables: "Is there anyone among you who, if your child asks for a fish, will give a snake instead of a fish? Or if the child asks for an egg, will give a scorpion? If you then, who are evil, know how to give good gifts to your children, how much more will the heavenly Father give the Holy Spirit to those who ask him!" (Luke 11:11–13). We only need to ask, but our asking must be matched by our readiness to receive.

In my early twenties, I went on a course called "Saints Alive" at my church. The early weeks built towards the sixth meeting when everyone was prayed for individually to be filled with the Holy Spirit. This time of prayer was pivotal for many of the participants, including me. As two of the course leaders prayed, I remember being overwhelmed with joy and feeling a strange warmth flood my body. As I was asked by the other members of the group about my experience, I recall struggling to put the experience into words, such was its depth. I still look back on that encounter with God as an important milestone on my journey, giving me a resolute confidence in God's closeness and love for me. My readiness to receive had been met by the generosity of God.

Our openness to God is a matter of desire and will. Desire: how much do we want to be filled with the Holy Spirit? Will: are we prepared to live in the power of the Spirit? Our readiness to receive the Spirit and to live in the power of the Spirit is fostered by the disciplines of the Christian life, and by cultivating an awareness of God whatever we are doing and wherever we are.

As we are filled with the Spirit, we are better able to live for God. As we live more faithfully, our capacity to receive the Spirit expands. Faithful discipleship—expressed in worship, prayer, and loving relationships and actions—empties us of selfishness and creates more space for the Spirit to fill. In turn, our lives are increasingly animated by the Spirit, and we become more responsive to the Spirit in our everyday experiences. There is a wonderful synergy here, in that our love for God and our capacity to receive the Holy Spirit grow together.

Whilst the Holy Spirit draws us into Christ, making our lives and Christ's ever more closely identified, we never lose our autonomy. We go on making choices for ourselves but we learn to conform to the Spirit's promptings as we follow Christ. Remember, God is committed to our uniqueness and upholds our integrity as an individual free to decide. Our freedom, though, is not impaired by aligning our life with Christ's. On the contrary, our freedom finds its fulfilment: we are set free to live for God and to realize our unique role in God's plans. In the Spirit, we are inspired to worship God and live for God, and by the Spirit, we are enabled to say "Yes" to God when God calls us to a particular task or into a specific relationship.

The Holy Spirit, Christ and the cross

It was Christ's self-offering on the cross that released the gift of the Holy Spirit. Jesus told his disciples on the night before he died, "Nevertheless, I tell you the truth: it is to your advantage that I go away, for if I do not go away, the Advocate will not come to you; but if I go, I will send him to you" (John 16:7). The life given by the Spirit is cross-shaped, a life given as we die to selfishness and live to God. When the Risen Christ breathes the Spirit into the disciples on the day of his resurrection, he sends them out to continue God's mission, having first shown them the wounds on his hands and his side (John 20:19–23). They, and we, can be in no doubt that as we venture out in mission, we have the authority and power of Christ but must also expect to be wounded and rejected, like Christ, the Crucified One.

This cruciform life requires our cooperation. We are to relinquish self-centred patterns of thought and behaviour, and embrace the self-giving, divine life, epitomized by the crucifixion of Christ. When we are selfish or do anything that is an offence against love, we thwart God's work in our lives, introducing a jarring dissonance to the harmony of our life with Christ's.

As we let go of the control of our lives and are renewed by the Holy Spirit, we are taken deeper into the Passion of Christ. In the weakness and obedience of the cross, we learn a deeper dependence on Christ. Only through being grounded in the love of Christ does our prayer and activity become fruitful: "My Father is glorified by this, that you bear much fruit and become my disciples. As the Father has loved me, so I love you; abide in my love" (John 15:8–9). When we share in Christ's life, we embrace his life of humble service and sacrificial love. Looking out for those on the edge of the various conversations over coffee at church or signing up to help in a charity shop or lobbying our Member of Parliament about climate change are examples of how we can identify with Christ, and serve his kingdom.

We respond to God's call to a "greater love"—sacrificial love by which we "lay down our lives" in the service of others—by attending to Christ and by cooperating with the Holy Spirit's work within us (John 15:12). This has always been the way of discipleship. In the early church, those first disciples were able to draw upon their own memories of seeing, touching and eating with Jesus to shape how they related to the Risen Christ in the power of the Spirit. Whereas we are separated in time by 2,000 years, we are informed by their accounts and reflections in the New Testament and have the same Spirit inspiring us, the same mandate, and the same desire as those first disciples: we seek to follow Christ so that he can be known and loved through us.

The Holy Spirit and the Church

Luke's account of the outpouring of the Holy Spirit in Acts 2 has parallels with the theophany—the coming of God—at Sinai in the Old Testament (Exodus 19:1–25; Deuteronomy 9:6–15). In Jerusalem, there was wind and fire; at Sinai, thunder and lightning. At Sinai, the people left the camp and were at the foot of the mountain where God descended; at Pentecost, those who believed in Jesus were together in one room when the Holy Spirit came down upon them. Luke is making it clear that the coming of the Holy Spirit on Jesus' first followers at Pentecost is another theophany. God has come to them to unite them and send them out on God's mission. Empowered by the Holy Spirit, they are propelled onto the streets of Jerusalem to proclaim the resurrection and vindication of Jesus, in the city where he had been crucified.

When I went for an interview at the Church Mission Society's headquarters in London in 1986, above the entrance was the Great Commission from the end of Mark's Gospel: "Go forth to every part of the world to proclaim the good news to the whole creation" (Mark 16:15). In Matthew's gospel, Jesus follows this great command with this promise, "Remember, I am with you always, to the end of the age" (Matthew 28:20). Whenever we leave our comfort zones and engage in mission, Christ is with us to strengthen and to guide.

Formed and inhabited by Christ, the Church shares in his relationship with the Father: we are God's children, bound together in God's life. Our birthright as children of God is to pray to the Father as Jesus did: "And because you are children, God has sent the Spirit of his Son into our hearts, crying, 'Abba! Father!'" (Galatians 4:6; see also Romans 8:14–17).

At the Eucharist, the Holy Spirit pervades the Church, consecrating the bread and wine, and the people of God. The confirmation of the Holy Spirit's presence is resurrection joy. Grounded in faith, hope and love, the Church knows in the Eucharist the exuberance of God's kingdom through the Spirit. As Pope Francis has said, "The identification card of the Christian is joy: the joy of the Gospel."[16] This is not the transient happiness of success but the ceaseless joy radiating from the Risen Christ who is with us. It is Mary's joy on hearing her name spoken by Jesus on that first Easter morning, and the exultant joy of the Easter shout, "Alleluia, Christ is risen!"

Our readiness to experience the ebullience of the Holy Spirit in the Eucharist depends on how we live day by day, week by week. Do we seek to live in the Spirit in the rest of our lives? Do we seek to love as Christ loves us? As what we profess in church matches up more closely with how we live, then our hearts are softened and our capacity for joy increases. In the Eucharist, our identity as God's children is renewed, and we go back into the world to live as children of God: our lives are to reflect our status as daughters and sons of God. As we better reflect the truth we experience in the Eucharist in our daily lives, our worship and our lives are progressively characterized by Christ's joy.

The Holy Spirit and the kingdom

In the Eucharist, the kingdom—the reign of God inaugurated by Christ—is present in our midst through the Holy Spirit. We are taken beyond this world into the kingdom of heaven where we know "peace and joy in the Holy Spirit" (Romans 14:17). Having experienced the kingdom, we know the dissonance between the world as it is and how God intends it to be, and our longing for the consummation of God's plan when God's kingdom will come on earth is heightened. We go from the Eucharist, therefore, energized to work for peace and justice, driven onwards by our anticipation of the coming of the kingdom. In each celebration of the Eucharist, the Spirit moulds the Church to be a more effective instrument of God's loving purposes in the world.

A prayer for the coming of the Holy Spirit

> Heavenly King, Comforter, Spirit of Truth, everywhere present, filling all things, Treasury of all Good and Giver of Life, come and dwell in us and cleanse us from sin, and of your goodness, heal our souls.[17]

CHAPTER 5

Living eucharistically

Rejoice always, pray without ceasing, give thanks in all circumstances; for this is the will of God in Christ Jesus for you.
1 Thessalonians 5:16–18

When I was ten, top of my Christmas present list was a racing bike. As soon as the Christmas displays had gone up in the shops at the beginning of October, I had begun my campaign. I told my mum and dad more than once that month, "If you are wondering about Christmas presents, my bike is in bad shape." In November, I mentioned something that was wrong with my current bike each week: "the frame is rusty," "sometimes the gears jump," "one of my mudguards has fallen off" and "the brakes are dodgy in the wet". When we got to December, I was just explicit: "I'd love a new bike, a five-gear racing bike." Cheekily I had specified the colour, red, and the make, Raleigh, and had left the relevant page of the catalogue open on the coffee table in the living room. When I spotted that mum had closed it and tucked it away on the shelf beneath, I would open it up and put it back on top for all to see.

Christmas Day dawned, and after a restless night, I crept downstairs before anyone else had woken, to see whether I had the present I wanted. The presents were always around the Christmas tree in the corner, but there was nothing among them that was bike-sized. Disappointed, I went back to bed to wait until it was time for us all to get up.

Having opened all our presents later that morning and with still no sign of the bike, Dad announced that there was one more "in the garage". I was excited, but part of me dared not believe that I was going to get the present I craved. A short while later, along with my younger sister, mum and dad, I was looking at an object concealed by an old sheet that looked to be exactly the right shape and size.

When dad pulled off the covering to reveal the bike, it was exactly what I wanted. I gazed admiringly, rapt in the pleasure of having it, and anticipating riding it to the shops and to the park. Then I awoke from my reverie, prompted by the question my mum or dad had asked me on previous similar occasions, sounding inside my head: "What do you say?"

I turned to my mum and dad: "Thank you. Thank you so much. It's perfect."

Thankfulness for our relationship with God

What defines a human being? In western culture, we tend to ask when we meet someone new, "What do you do?" By contrast, when I lived in Uganda in my mid-twenties, the getting-to-know-you enquiries centred on your family, and I would respond, "I have a sister called Ann; my parents are Bob and Vera." In that culture, people were less interested in what others did, and more concerned with who they knew and where they fitted in the network of relationships. This emphasis on relationships was further reflected in the importance of hospitality in the hierarchy of values; it was pretty much at the top of the list. Whenever anyone visited your home, you had to invite them over the threshold, give them a cup of tea and something to eat, never mind if you were doing something else, however important it might be. The task at hand was always secondary to the person standing at the door. On the way home from the school where I taught or the local market, you had to stop and chat with anyone you knew. Otherwise, you would be regarded as rude and antisocial. You were encouraged to go and see your neighbours and friends when you had some free time. What mattered most to the local people was our readiness to visit people, to chat when out and about, and to receive guests in our home. In that culture, what we did was secondary to who we were, and that was believed to be seen most clearly in how we related to the others in the community where we were set. The value we placed on those relationships was determined by the locals by how much time we gave to them. A pithy saying summarized neatly this difference between the two value systems, "You have watches but we have time." Behind this cultural difference is what may be a universal truth: that the greatest gift we can give someone else is our time and attention.

For Christians, the fundamental relationship is with God. This relationship can be construed in three distinct ways. Firstly, we are creatures utterly dependent on the Creator, who gives us life itself and all we need to sustain life. Since we have chosen to ignore this reality and seek to live independently of God, we are, though, sinners. Secondly, through Christ, we are forgiven sinners. Finally, in Christ, we share in the Son's relationship with the Father, and are children of God. We are then creatures, forgiven sinners, and children of God, and each of these ways in which we relate to God gives us reasons to be thankful.

Thankfulness for creation

In our celebration of the Eucharist, we affirm that life is eucharistic, a gift from God and a cause for thanksgiving. My tutor at theological college once relayed how a neighbour, a landscape painter, had started asking him about the interface between art and faith. He sensed that this was not just an intellectual enquiry but reflected his search for God. After many conversations, the eventual breakthrough from agnosticism to a belief that there is a God came one day when the artist was on holiday in the USA. He was on a long, sweeping road in New England. Trees in their rich autumn colours lined the route, hills rose in the distance, the sunshine was bright, and the sky cloudless and an intense blue. Enjoying the breathtaking beauty of the scene, a simple thought popped unexpectedly into his head: "Why is there anything here at all?" He was then overcome by a sense of wonder that the world existed, and he was alive. Overwhelmed with gratitude, he stopped to give thanks, even though he was not sure to whom he was grateful. This kind of thankfulness for the gift of life and creation is woven into the fabric of the Eucharist.

Thankfulness for God's provision

As creatures, we realize that the whole of life—food, work, rest and leisure—is a gift from God. The appropriate response to this gift is to give thanks, particularly for God's provision of food and water, essential for life. God's generous provision of food and drink to all his creatures is poetically conveyed by the psalmist, "These all look to you to give them their food in due season; when you give to them, they gather it up; when you open your hand, they are filled with good things" (Psalm 104:27–8).

One obvious opportunity to express our thankfulness for God's provision is at meals, which can begin with a simple prayer of thanks for the gifts of God that are shared at the table. This can be quite simple, for example, "Father, thank you for this food and all your gifts to us, Amen." Amusing variations can add some humour, for example, "Bless this bunch as they munch their lunch." When I was working in the USA at a Salvation Army summer camp after graduation, the customary prayer before meals was, "Be present at our table, Lord; be here and everywhere adored; these mercies bless, and grant that we may strengthened for thy service be. Amen." Whatever prayer we use, the key is that the giver of the gifts of food and drink is acknowledged and thanked. The psalmist urges God's people to "offer to God a sacrifice of thanksgiving" and God underlines the importance of gratitude in the same psalm: "Those who bring thanksgiving as their sacrifice honour me" (Psalm 50).

Meals together are much more than an opportunity to eat and drink. Sharing a meal gives those gathered a chance to talk together and express their care for each other. The maxim "families that eat together stay together" is simplistic but reflects the value of being together around a table enjoying food and drink, and each other's company. In the conversation that flows, everyone is to ensure that all have the chance to contribute and no one dominates. By talking and listening to each other graciously everyone feels valued, and the shared love around the table, as well as our bodies, is nourished.

Being thankful each time we eat and drink reminds us that we are creatures, dependent on God. This simple act of gratitude reflects God's purposes for humanity because we are called to receive life as a gift from God, and offer it back to God with thanksgiving. Life and the world around us are gifts, sustained by God's love. Humanity's role is to offer creation back to the Father with thanksgiving. This can be described as a priestly role because it is taking what has been given, the food and drink at a meal for instance, and offering it for God's blessing. This understanding is reflected in another prayer for use before meals, "Bless this food to our use, and ourselves in your service."

As well as our priestly function of offering creation back to the Father thankfully, we all have a reconciling ministry too. We are to heal any divisions and strengthen the life of any community to which we belong, seeking harmony wherever we are. Collaborating with the work of the Holy Spirit, who strives to bring us into interdependent relationships of love, we are to do whatever we can to contribute to the fulfilment of the vision of humanity united in love for each other and love for God.

All that exists is God's gift: its purpose is to make God known to humanity, and to make humanity's life communion with God. Creation is the sign and means of God's presence, wisdom and love; it offers an invitation: "O taste and see that the Lord is good" (Psalm 34:8).

In knowing God's love in the eating of bread and drinking of wine in the Eucharist, we affirm that each meal and every aspect of life can be an experience of God's love. The wine we drink on other occasions and the food on our plate at home are also tangible—and, hopefully, flavoursome—manifestations of God's love. As we grow in faith, we gradually begin to respond to all of life in gratitude and find all we experience—even the heartache and sorrows—as an opportunity to draw closer to God. Thus, our life can become a continuously unbroken relationship with God. Our entire lives can be sacramental—a means of encountering God—and characterized by thanksgiving, when we see all we receive—food and drink, love and laughter, family and friends—as a gift, and offer these gifts back to God thankfully.

We worship God in church, in order that our entire lives become worship. When we offer our experience in church and out of church to God, the whole of life becomes an opportunity to know and love God. Sin can be defined as the opposite: taking what God gives and keeping it for ourselves. Life then becomes closed off from God, sapped of vitality and stripped of meaning. When individuals persistently pursue their own agenda and ignore God, they close their minds and hearts to life's transcendent dimension, and distance themselves from love and life. We are to choose to receive life from God and know God's blessing, and to respond thankfully (Deuteronomy 30:19).

Thankfulness for God's grace

As well as being God's creatures, we are also "forgiven sinners". The cross means that there are no sins that are not already forgiven. When we grasp this truth, we are overcome with gratitude and astounded by God's generous grace. This insight gives rise to great joy and the issuing of an invitation to others to rejoice with us. As we discover in each of Jesus' parables in Luke 15, our elation at the extravagance of God's love parallels the delight in heaven when someone turns to God. Jesus tells these three stories to explain why he is eating and drinking with "tax collectors and sinners", instead of shunning them as his opponents do. They believe that to make it clear that they disapprove of the tax collectors' and sinners' behaviour, they must ostracize them. Beneath their querulous attitude towards Jesus are two incisive questions about his willingness to receive the hospitality of these wrongdoers, "Do you not realize how bad these people are? Or do you not care?" A "yes" to either question would undermine Jesus' credentials as a prophet.

Each of these parables has a similar pattern: something is lost, a sheep, a coin and a son. The leading character finds what is lost and hosts a feast for the entire community to celebrate. Jesus tells his listeners that the joy of those who celebrate in the stories is matched in heaven when one sinner repents. These parables tell us that when we respond with open hands and a soft heart to God's offer of grace, God's relentless love surges into joy that is both God's and ours. This is mirrored in our experience: God's joy resonates with our jubilation. Whenever we understand the magnitude of God's mercy and know that our sins are forgiven, our gratitude erupts into joy, like a jet of champagne that flies out of the shaken bottle when the cork pops out.

The call to give thanks remains even when life is dark and difficult, for God is still present and remains faithful. By giving thanks at the Last Supper, Jesus connects one of the darkest places of human experience with God the giver. On the night when he is betrayed and facing his own death, Jesus blesses God for the bread and wine. In front of those around the table, he affirms again that God is the Creator and the Giver of life. By this simple but profound act of offering thanks, he renews his faith in God and finds that his resolve to embrace God's unfolding future is strengthened.

When we, like Jesus, are facing an ordeal, we too can remember this consoling truth: God is with us and is always faithful. We can look around and see God's presence, perhaps in an offer of help, in newfound strength to cope, or in God's gifts of food, loving relationships, and the beauty of creation, and continue to give thanks. God's unfailing generosity whatever the circumstances is the reason to be thankful.

While we seek to receive all of life from God and offer it back to God, we need to remember that everything that happens does not come directly from God. We are not fatalists who believe that every event in the world is orchestrated by God. Our response to tragedy and suffering is not to be a rueful, yet resigned acceptance. I have sometimes heard people say, "This has happened for a reason" or "This must be part of God's plan" in response to sickness or tragic deaths or a natural disaster or a pandemic. There is an important distinction to be made between God bringing something good out of a devastating situation and believing that God has been instrumental in a personal or national catastrophe. Otherwise, we can end up with a distorted image of God, capricious and careless, and certainly far from Christlike. Therefore, we thank God not for the crisis but in the crisis, whether it is global, national, or local and personal. By giving thanks whatever life brings, and offering back to God every experience, however agonizing, we begin to see that God can bring some good even out of the most unlikely of events (Romans 8:28).

When our lives have their daily challenges, we can still be grateful. In my time teaching in Uganda, I was struck by the Christians' thankfulness to God for the gift of life, despite their relative poverty and struggles to stay healthy. Even when grieving we can find reasons to be thankful. On many funeral visits, I have found those bereaved grateful for the cards and other expressions of love that they have received, a cause for thanksgiving to God.

When we are so depressed that we are blind to God's goodness, the discipline of giving thanks can help lift us, if only a little, from our despondency. Sometimes giving thanks can feel like an act of faith. Determining to give thanks, even when we do not feel like it, sustains our faith, and pleases God. I remember breaking one of my toys and my mum trying to fix it but to no avail. Nevertheless, I muttered, "Thanks anyway, Mum," through my sobs and that meant a lot to her. When we offer our experience—whatever it is—to God with thanksgiving, we are learning to live eucharistically, for we are obeying the injunction to "do everything in the name of the Lord Jesus, giving thanks to God the Father through him" (Colossians 3:17).

Giving thanks in the Father's presence

In the Eucharist, alongside our rejoicing in the goodness of God shown in creation, we celebrate the advent of God's kingdom, the reign of God, in Christ. We are convinced that the kingdom of God is here because the Risen Christ is in our midst. Where the Risen Christ is, there is the Father and the Holy Spirit too; the Holy Trinity is the source and goal of the life of each eucharistic community. In the Eucharist, we participate in the rhythm of Christ's joyful return to the Father in the power of the Spirit, and find that we are in the Father's presence. Sharing in the Son's relationship with the Father, and as daughters and sons of God, we feel the Holy Spirit stirring us to cry out to God, "Our Father".

As Christ shares his last meal with his friends, he determines that the bread— "this is my body"—and the wine—"this is my blood"—be identified with him. When the bread and wine representing Christ are offered back to the Father in the Eucharist, Christ's return to the Father via his death, resurrection and ascension is symbolized. In John's Gospel, this is seen as one upward movement, from his being lifted up in crucifixion through resurrection to his return to the Father's presence in heaven. In the Eucharistic Prayer, we are taken on this same journey with Christ through the cross and resurrection into the Father's presence. When we all affirm our participation in this great prayer of praise and thanksgiving in the climactic "Amen", we are in the kingdom of God, face to face with the Father, and ready to pray boldly, "Our Father . . . ". Here we delight in being God's children. With our brother, Christ, we face the Father "lost in wonder, love, and praise".[18]

Offering the whole of our lives to God in gratitude

Sharing in the intimacy of the Son's relationship with the Father in the Eucharist, we strive in the power of the Holy Spirit to emulate the Son's responsiveness to the Father throughout our lives. We aspire to fulfil the Father's purpose that we be "conformed to the image of his Son" (Romans 8:29). This is a demanding transformation and one we meet slowly over time as step by step we become more Christlike. When we struggle to grow into maturity, we can be comforted by knowing that Jesus Christ also found obedience to God stretching. Whilst Jesus Christ made the perfect response to God, with every second of every day lived obediently, he was nevertheless tempted. Following his baptism, Jesus was taunted by the devil, and presented with three ways to avoid the cross: instead of being crucified, he could be a self-serving, spectacular or political messiah. We can speculate that Jesus might have hesitated for a moment as he experienced the lure of an easier route ahead (Matthew 4:1–11; Luke 4:1–13). Also, in the Garden of Gethsemane, Jesus wrestles with the inevitability of crucifixion, praying three times, "My Father, if it is possible, let this cup pass from me; yet not what I want but what you want" (Matthew 26:36–46). Through these times of testing, Jesus' love for the Father is taken to a deeper level, and he remoulds our humanity. By resisting selfishness, Christ recasts humanity, making it cruciform and full of love. This new humanity is given to us in Christ.

The final reshaping of our distorted humanity and the consummation of Jesus' love for the Father are achieved in the fire of the Paschal Mystery. On the cross, as Jesus drinks the dregs of the cup of suffering, his self-offering reaches its high point. This climactic surrender to God in love defines Christ's life for eternity. His life of obedience, love and thanksgiving to God—his eucharistic life—is now given to us in baptism and by faith. This participation in Christ's life is captured in the simple biblical designation of being "in Christ" (2 Corinthians 5:17). "In Christ" our lives are renewed (as Christ fills us with himself) that we might know his presence and his love everywhere and always.

The bread—which "earth has given and human hands have made"—and wine—"fruit of the vine and work of human hands"—offered in the Eucharist represents the totality of creation and all human endeavour.[19] The wheat and the grapes are harvested but need human ingenuity to become bread and wine. In the offering of the bread and wine, we too are included: we are offered and taken into the ceaseless self-offering of Christ. As Augustine of Hippo famously said, "It is you who lie upon the altar; it is you, your very life within the cup."[20] As we offer the bread and wine, we give ourselves, our complete bodily life, to be a "living sacrifice" (Romans 12:1–2). The bread and wine are taken by Christ, transformed into symbols of his body and blood, and offered to the Father. Thereby, the bread and wine that represent our lives become symbols of Christ's life; our offering is integrated into Christ's self-offering. The symbolism of our lives being subsumed into the symbolism of Christ's self-giving conveys the staggering and wonderful truth that we and the whole of Creation are included in Christ's self-offering to the Father. As Christ gives himself to the Father on the cross, he offers us and our lives, the whole of humanity and the entire created order to the Father for eternity: you and I are integral to this gift.

A renewed creation

In Christ, the entire creation is renewed. As Jesus gives himself finally and fully to the Father on the cross, he gathers the whole of creation and offers it back to God. Jesus releases all that is his, the created order, and his life into the Father's hands. His letting go of life at the point of death is the culmination of a life of self-giving love. "All things have been created through him and for him ... and through him God was pleased to reconcile to himself all things, whether on earth or in heaven, by making peace through the blood of his cross" (Colossians 1:16–20). A line from Graham Kendrick's song "The Servant King" underlines the link between the Christ through whom creation comes into being and the Christ who died on a cross outside the walls of Jerusalem: "Hands that flung stars into space to cruel nails surrendered." Besides humanity finding its fulfilment in Christ, the rest of creation does too. In Christ, all creation finds its being, its life and its purpose.

Through Christ, we are the children of God. As we participate in Christ's life by receiving life from and returning it to God with thanksgiving, life is transformed into an exchange of love with God. Life becomes communion again. In the story of the Fall, Adam and Eve took the "fruit of the tree that is in the middle of the garden" and ate it (Genesis 3:3–6). The end of the eating was the enjoyment of the fruit; it was not a means of relating in love to God, because God had explicitly told them not to eat it. In the new creation in Christ, there is a new pattern to our lives: God gives life to us in Christ, and we receive and return the gift in gratitude in Christ.

Any remaining self-centred patterns of thought or behaviour distract and dull us to Christ's presence. When we fall back into selfish attitudes or self-centred actions, Christ remains present but we are absent. In the imagery of the parable of the Prodigal Son: Christ remains at home, but we have gone to the far country (Luke 15:11–32).

Christ is always attentive to us with his gaze steady and fixed. Seeking our full attention and our ready response, Christ faces us. At our baptism, we promise to turn away from sin, to repent, and turn to Christ. This is not a one-off but an ongoing commitment. We need to look to Christ as Christ looks at us, faithfully and with love.

To deny or ignore Christ's presence is to carry on in the same old way and to bear its consequences. That is what Paul meant when he told us that "the wages of sin is death, but the free gift of God is eternal life in Christ Jesus our Lord" (Romans 6:23). In response to Christ, we re-orientate ourselves, turning away from sin—all that mars our own life and the life of the community to which we belong—and towards Christ. By putting our faith in Christ, we know the power of the Holy Spirit, which enables us to follow Christ and to be thankful to God. As we receive with gratitude what God has done for us in Christ and what God is giving us in the here and now, we experience the abundant life Christ gives us. To enable us to be consistently re-orientating ourselves and readjusting our priorities to the truth that Christ is here in our midst, God has given us the Eucharist.

God has given us the Eucharist to sustain and energize our love for God

My prayer triplet has been meeting twice a year for the last twenty-five years in Cambridge, where we met at theological college. Our get-togethers there follow a familiar pattern. We have lunch, followed by coffee at a nearby café. Then we pray in a church in the centre of the city before rounding off the afternoon with tea and a piece of cake. This pattern of meeting in the spring and autumn, alongside twenty-four hours together in the summer on the coast of Norfolk, has been good. Our increasing resemblance to the three characters in the TV series *The Last of the Summer Wine*—a whimsical comedy that features three likeable retirees who while away the time together mischievously and reflectively—indicates how relaxed we are in each company and how we are all getting older. For those who know the characters, we have not risked having a conversation about who most resembles Compo, the comic figure who never took off his welly boots or his woollen hat, and was always broke. Our meeting up to catch up and to pray together strengthens our commitment to each other. These times together sustain our longstanding friendship. In between, we keep in touch and continue to pray for each other, but we look forward to our get-togethers. It is what we experience intensely together that defines our friendship and deepens our ongoing love for each other. Similarly, when the Church comes together to celebrate the Eucharist, this powerful experience of closeness to one another and to God intensifies our love for God, and for each other. Between Eucharists, the love we have experienced together is then shared with those in the places to which we are dispersed, our homes, our work settings, in our neighbourhoods, wherever we are.

The Eucharist animates and relates our lives to God. As we participate in Christ's life, every aspect of life becomes shot through with the presence of God. Through his incarnation, Christ has embraced every feature of life from birth to death, making life a unified whole. This means that the life that we are offered in Christ is one life without division or fragmentation. Whereas we tend to divide life up into various dichotomies, the profane and the sacred, the natural and the supernatural, the religious and the secular, the spiritual and the material, Christ draws our lives into a coherent whole. These false oppositions that plague contemporary understandings of life effectively hive off parts of life—the profane, the natural, the secular and the material—and assert that they do not belong to God. This is not a new feature of the way we understand the world. There has been for some time talk of the "God of the gaps"—God as the explanation of various phenomena when science cannot provide one. However, as scientific knowledge increased, the space left for God correspondingly shrank.

All these ways of separating life into two categories, only one of which is God's, are not true to the Christ who is at the centre of creation and who enfolds the whole of our lives. Christians must resist the pressure to collude with the view that God is concerned primarily with the Church and our private devotion. We must resist attempts to push God to the margins because God is passionately engaged with every aspect of life, and our relationship with Christ encompasses our entire lives.

The Church gathers for worship and disperses in mission

While our prayer and worship are our top priority, the authenticity of our relationship with God is tested by our subsequent engagement in God's mission to the world. The Church sets aside sacred spaces, churches and chapels, in order that we may learn to see the whole world as sacred. We label some experiences as "supernatural" because they defy our expectations, but the totality of life remains God's. Our religious practice is not an escape but a preparation to relate to people and organizations beyond the Church with insight and energy. Mindful that this is God's creation, and with the incarnation of God in Christ central to our understanding of life and the world, we are to see that our search for meaning enfolds the entire created order and every person we encounter. We serve God who is the God of the Church and the golf club, the God of the chapel and the cinema, the God of prayer and politics, the God of worship and work. Each time we celebrate the Eucharist, we offer ourselves to serve God by seeking justice and peace. When we gather, we bring the whole of humanity and the entire created order to God in prayer. Belonging to God's Church means that we long for the kingdom of God to come and for that unity in love which is God's goal for his creation. We go from the Eucharist to put that longing into practice, in our words and actions, wherever we are and whatever we are doing.

While each church has its own distinctive history and identity, and a mission and ministry informed by its context, every church bears witness to the same Christ. In the Eucharist, Christ judges our infidelity to God, purifies and unites us, and sends us out. Dispersed in the world, we sustain the prayer of the Church by attending to Christ wherever we are, praying for each other, and giving thanks for God's goodness. Thereby the Church's responsiveness to Christ and its chorus of gratitude, renewed in the Eucharist, is ceaseless. As John Ellerton, a vicar in the nineteenth century, wrote in his evening hymn, "The day thou gavest, Lord, is ended": "The voice of prayer is never silent, nor dies the strain of praise away."

Prayer

> I thank thee, God, that I have lived in this great
>   world and known its many joys:
> The songs of birds, the strongest sweet scent of hay,
> And cooling breezes in the secret dusk;
> The flaming sunsets at the close of day,
> Hills and the lovely, heather-covered moors;
> Music at night, and the moonlight on the sea,
> The beat of waves upon the rocky shore
> And wild white spray, flung high in ecstasy;
> The faithful eyes of dogs, and treasured books,
> The love of kin and fellowship of friends
> And all that makes life dear and beautiful.
> I thank Thee too, that there has come to me a
>   little sorrow and sometimes defeat,
> A little heartache and the loneliness that comes
>   with parting and the words "Good-bye";
> Dawn breaking after weary hours of pain,
> When I discovered that night's gloom must yield and
>   morning light break through to me again.

Because of these and other blessings poured
    unasked upon my wondering head,
Because I know that there is yet to come an
    even richer and more glorious life,
And most of all, because Thine only Son once
    sacrificed life's loveliness for me,
I thank Thee, God, that I have lived.

Elizabeth Craven[21]

CHAPTER 6

Communion

The grace of the Lord Jesus Christ, the love of God, and the communion of the Holy Spirit be with all of you.
2 Corinthians 13:13

One Sunday morning, I went to St Martin's Church in the Bullring in Birmingham before catching the train at the nearby New Street Station. I was warmly welcomed at the door by the priest who was going to preside and directed to the side chapel, where several people were already sitting chatting quietly to each other. By the time the service started, those gathered reflected this multi-ethnic city and its wealth disparities too. We were a diverse group, yet one in our common humanity and in God's love. As we stood in a semi-circle around the altar ready to receive, I looked around at the faces of the people there with me. One or two looked tired, others strained, and some calm. Our disparate lives connected at this point of stillness and expectation. Before our shared need of God's grace and mercy, our differences faded away. As we proffered our hands and opened our mouths to receive, we were one. Our unity was not generated by us, although we had played our part by praying the liturgy, singing, and assembling at the altar. It was a gift, and in that gift, we had been given a foretaste of heaven. In our oneness, we had shared an experience of transcendence: we had participated in holy communion.

Baptism the guarantee of communion

Communion is defined by the relationship within the Godhead between Father, Son and Holy Spirit. The triune God is the Father, Son and Holy Spirit, in an intimate relationship of love and mutual dependence. This closeness is not exclusive like a tight-knit friendship group which struggles to include anyone new. Quite the reverse: there is always space for someone else to join; there is always room for one more. To use an analogy, it is the absolute opposite of the children's party game musical chairs where each time the music stops a chair is taken away and someone drops out; as soon as the chairs are filled, another is added, ready for the next person to join. Rublev's famous icon of the Trinity depicts this limitless invitation to communion with the seat in the foreground ready for you to occupy in the presence of the Father, Son and Holy Spirit.

There is always a place for anyone to join because God's hospitality is radically inclusive. All we need to do is say "Yes" to the standing invitation in Christ addressed to everyone: "Come and enjoy divine hospitality. Come and revel in eternal love." When we allow ourselves to be caught up in the love of God, we discover a love for each other which transcends any other experience of togetherness.

Baptism is the supreme marker of our unity and the guarantee of communion. As one Body, we are baptized into the death and resurrection of Christ.[22] His death sealed an eternal relationship between God and God's people, who are no longer ethnically defined but are identified solely by allegiance to Christ, with baptism as the rite of entry into this community centred on Christ.

The cross is the foundation of our shared life into which we are initiated in our baptism. With each successive step of faith, we are taken deeper into Christ, sharing in his death and resurrection. Dying and rising with Christ, we share his life with our brothers and sisters in the Holy Spirit. Christ's life animates our entire lives, and through us revitalizes our weary neighbours and our tired world.

In the Eucharist, each of us finds that our uniqueness is cherished, and, at the same time, our love for each other expressed and deepened. Our unity is not uniformity or conformity: our unity does not deny our singularity—there is only one of you—and affirms the differences between us, delighting in our diversity. Through our relationship with God and each other within the Church, we discover who we are, finding our authentic identity. Instead of being trapped by how we were labelled at school or what we have been told by various authority figures within the family or at work, we are set free to discover who we were created to be, to find our gifts and our role within the life of God's Church and in God's plan for the world.

Communion is the defining feature of God's Church

Our communion is expressed in our worship, our joint activities—weekends away, harvest suppers and Bible study groups—and as we weep and celebrate together. Communion flows from our allegiance to Christ, which surpasses all other commitments. Every other loyalty—family, ethnic, tribal or national—is secondary to our primary loyalty to Christ. While our life in Christ is joyful, it can be costly too. We share in Christ's sufferings, persecution and his mission (2 Corinthians 1:7). We participate in Christ's death and resurrection, the defining feature and the touchstone of our discipleship. We cannot enjoy resurrection without knowing death; they are inseparable as we follow Christ. To rise, we must die.

Only when the church in Jerusalem faced harsh persecution did it finally fulfil Jesus' command to be his witnesses beyond the city in which its members lived. Fleeing the threat of martyrdom, the first disciples of Jesus ventured beyond the city walls into Judea and Samaria, but this did not mean they would be safe (Acts 8:1). Paul often cited the dangers he faced from bandits, political authorities and religious opponents, in the wilderness and at sea, not as unexpected hazards but as his credentials. He regarded his suffering as the authenticating mark of his missionary calling. For Christians in the comfortable West, it can be a struggle even to risk embarrassment by opening up a conversation about what we believe or offering a biblical perspective on a topical issue, such as the fate of refugees or the mounting numbers of children living in poverty around us. Mission, whether it means crossing geographical borders or cultures, or crossing the room to talk to a stranger, is bound to make us feel exposed, for we do not know in advance how we will be received. This vulnerability is an encounter with the cross, which we always find when we engage in mission.

The Church's mission and common life are fashioned by the cross. Keeping Christ's crucifixion central to our corporate life reminds us of our common standing before God: we are all sinners. Yet we are forgiven because of the cross and our capacity to receive grace. Conscious of our sin and rejoicing in the grace that we have received, we share in God's mission to the world. We long for all those we meet to know Christ, who is drawing us and them into the love and life of the triune God.

Through Christ we share in the glory of God

Since the humanity of Christ is the gateway to union with God, we find in the Eucharist that our senses, our desires, our imaginations—all that constitutes our humanity—are instrumental in our worship. As we give ourselves to God through the liturgy, we are soaked in the Holy Spirit and renewed in God's love which God pours into our hearts (Romans 5:5). Our witness to Christ beyond the Church is energized through the joy and love we experience in the Eucharist. Having been recalled to the sacrificial, self-giving life of Christ, we go on to respond to and reveal God's love in the world.

By sharing God's love week in and week out, we become more Christlike. Our communion with God and our brothers and sisters in God's Church deepens as we live and love faithfully. By God's grace at work in us, we are "conformed to the image of his Son." (Romans 8:29) This work of the Holy Spirit steadily transforms our humanity until God's purpose is realized, and it, in the words of St Maximus the Confessor, a monk in the seventh century, "shines forth with a supernatural light and is transported above its own limits by a superabundance of glory".[23] Alleluia and Amen.

Prayer

Father of all,
we give you thanks and praise,
that when we were still far off
you met us in your Son and brought us home.
Dying and living, he declared your love,
gave us grace, and opened the gate of glory.
May we who share Christ's body live his risen life;
we who drink his cup bring life to others;
we whom the Spirit lights give light to the world.
Keep us firm in the hope you have set before us,
so we and all your children shall be free,
and the whole earth live to praise your name;
through Christ our Lord.
Amen.[24]

CHAPTER 7

Seeing Christ in everyday life

Those who eat my flesh and drink my blood abide in me, and I in them.
John 6:56

When I was nine years old, my father went to work in the Philippines for the World Health Organization for six weeks. While he was away, I had been captivated by the FA Cup Final, a dramatic and feisty game between Leeds and Chelsea that had ended in a two-all draw, necessitating a replay. I had been so enthralled by the match that I wanted to tell my dad all about it and wrote him a long letter, describing the moves that led to the four goals, and conveying the nail-biting uncertainty about the outcome right up until the final whistle. I started the letter with a gentle enquiry about how he was and rounded it off by letting him know that I, along with my mum and sister, were missing him. My dad kept this letter as a symbol of a particular stage in our relationship and our enduring love for each other.

Life is symbolic

Symbols, such as this letter that I sent my father, are integral to human interactions, helping us to express ourselves and build relationships. Symbols are sometimes denigrated as "mere signs", but to dismiss them in this way is to miss the distinction between a sign which points to another reality—a nearby town or hospital—and a symbol that expresses the reality to which it refers. Presenting a bouquet of flowers or a bottle of wine to the singers at the end of a concert conveys the appreciation of the audience, rather than simply pointing to it.

My wedding ring is a symbol of my marriage. When I notice it, I am taken back to my wedding day and to the church where I was married. The ring was blessed as a symbol of "unending love and faithfulness" and represents the reality of my marriage. It is also a public statement: anyone seeing this symbol knows that I am married. This symbol helps those I meet to make sense of my life and who I am, giving them genuine knowledge about me.

Lasting symbols make a statement about the meaning and shape of our lives, the fundamental relationships that define us. They help us to know and understand someone, and the world to which they belong. This kind of knowledge is sometimes called "knowledge by acquaintance" and is contrasted with "knowledge by description". To explain the difference between these two ways of knowing, let us think about a visit to the city of Paris. Ahead of a visit, I might read about the places to see and look at photographs of the major sights. This background work gives me information about Paris before I go there. I know Paris indirectly through the writing and the pictures of the key attractions. This is descriptive knowledge. When I am standing by the River Seine looking at the Eiffel Tower or eating at a restaurant in Montmartre, I am encountering Paris directly. I see its sights, hear its sounds, taste its food and drink its wine. I know for myself, not through someone else's report, that Paris is a wonderful city. This is called "knowledge by acquaintance". Or think of the difference between reading Michelle Obama's autobiography, *Becoming*, and meeting her in person; the former knowledge is indirect and the latter direct. Symbols mediate to us the reality of a place, a person or a relationship. They give us a direct encounter. We meet the truth to which they point.

Bread and wine are symbols of life

The bread and wine we offer and consume in the Eucharist are universal symbols. Across the globe, they represent life; as such their symbolism includes every facet of our material circumstances, everything that gives shape and content to our lives. From a Christian perspective, life and all that sustains it is a continuing gift from God. Therefore, these symbols, bread and wine, represent to us our lives in relationship to God, the giver.

Closely linked to their correspondence with life in general, bread and wine represent the food that we need to live: without food and drink, we die. In the Bible though, food and drink are not just sustenance; they are given for our enjoyment. God gives food to humanity for nourishment and pleasure, a means of relating in love to God. Food is God's love made tangible and tasty. In response to the love symbolized by the food, humanity is to reciprocate by loving God and to express that love through being thankful. The psalmist urges God's people to know God's goodness through creation: "You . . . bring forth food from the earth, and wine to gladden the human heart, oil to make the face shine, and bread to strengthen the human heart" (Psalm 104:14–15).

Creation is a sacrament

When God's people respond to what they taste and see by praising God, then God's love in creation realizes its goal. The waiting Father finds his love returned and the purpose of creation is accomplished.[25] The world is designed to be sacramental, to be a gift, given, received and returned to God in love. To be blind to this truth is to miss God's intention and resist God's overtures of love, for God is the "lover of humanity" and the world his gift. When we deny the world its sacramentality, we constrict our experience of God's love.[26] If we succumb to the prevailing tendency to divide life into natural—mundane, ordinary and typified by God's absence—and supernatural—occasional, extraordinary and defined as "acts of God"—our relationship with God is weakened.

Gerard Manley Hopkins recognizes the sacramentality of nature and humanity's blindness to it in his poem "God's Grandeur":

> The world is charged with the grandeur of God.
> It will flame out, like shining from shook foil;
> It gathers to a greatness, like the ooze of oil
> Crushed. Why do men then now not reck his rod?
> Generations have trod, have trod, have trod;

> And all is seared with trade; bleared, smeared with toil;
> And wears man's smudge and shares man's smell: the soil
> Is bare now, nor can foot feel, being shod.
>
> And for all this, nature is never spent;
> There lives the dearest freshness deep down things;
> And though the last lights off the black West went
> Oh, morning, at the brown brink eastward, springs—
> Because the Holy Ghost over the bent
> World broods with warm breast and with ah! bright wings.[27]

To split life into spheres of the sacred—God's territory—and the profane—the devil's domain—is to limit God's grace, and to deny God's sovereignty over the whole of creation. Our understanding of God's goodness and grace must be holistic: God's love enfolds the created order absolutely.

R. S. Thomas, the Welsh priest and poet, saw the glory of God in the world about us. He knows too, though, that we sometimes miss it. We can be absorbed by our petty preoccupations or caught up in the helter-skelter pace with which we move from one activity to another. To notice the glory of God that surrounds us, he tells us that we must learn to live in the eternal present, and take time to stop and look. We are not to reside in the past or wonder about the future but live in the moment that God is giving. The present moment is, after all, all we have:

> Life is not hurrying
> on to a receding future, nor hankering after
> an imagined past. It is the turning
> aside like Moses to the miracle
> of the lit bush, to a brightness
> that seemed as transitory as your youth
> once but is the eternity that awaits you.[28]

As we are so used to being in a hurry, and our typical attention span seems to be dwindling because of the hyper-stimulation of social media and the internet, we need even more to be reminded to take time to "stand and stare".[29]

Symbols of a renewed creation

The human skills of the baker and vintner, the gifts of grapes and the wheat, and the essential nature of bread and the celebratory function of wine in many cultures make bread and wine symbols of God's goodness in creation. In the Eucharist, saturated by the Holy Spirit, the bread and wine become symbols too of God's grace lavished upon us in Christ, and so represent to us the coming kingdom when creation will be renewed and suffused by the Spirit. Therefore, the bread and wine offered in the Eucharist become the epiphany, the revelation, of the new creation.

The one bread and one cup unite us in the Body of Christ, the Church

Through eating bread and drinking wine in the Eucharist, we know all the richness of our salvation won for us on the cross—grace, forgiveness, love, joy and peace—in our lives and our life together. Through this holy food and drink, we participate in Christ. Through the Holy Spirit, the bread and wine become to us the body and blood of Christ offered once for all on the cross but now in sacramental form. In receiving his body and blood, we know his life. Jesus said, "Unless you eat the flesh of the Son of Man and drink his blood, you have no life in you" (John 6:53).

To know Christ's life, we must be willing to embrace the cost of Christian discipleship, the experience of his death. Each time we eat Christ's body and drink Christ's blood in the Eucharist, we determine and declare our readiness to follow Christ whatever the cost. We recommit ourselves to ongoing, radical discipleship, for by eating from the plate and drinking from the cup, we are taken deeper into Christ's death. By eating his body and drinking his blood, we experience his dying. In consuming the bread and wine, we take his death at Calvary almost two thousand years ago—for us in history—within us.

At the Last Supper, Jesus took the cup, saying, "This cup that is poured out for you is the new covenant in my blood" (Luke 22:20). Jesus contrasts the new with the old covenant: both are underwritten in blood, but the new covenant is eternal (Exodus 24:3–8). By his death, Christ promises to love and cherish us "for better, for worse, for richer, for poorer, in sickness and in health, for ever".[30] Through our love for Christ and Christ's love for us, our hearts, minds, and wills are united with his, and we gradually become one with Christ. We begin to share one life, and our identities start to coincide.

This close relationship and overlapping of identities between Christ and his Church struck me at an evening service led by the young people of a church in Saffron Walden. Its theme was "persevering in discipleship". In our reflection around our tables, we were asked to consider, "How are we inspired by Jesus' example?" This question got me thinking and I concluded that there are two levels at which it can be addressed. One answer sees Christ as separate from us, as the supremely inspirational figure who we seek to copy. With this view, we try to match Christ's determination to persevere. We strive, like him, to be obedient to God's unfolding plan for us whatever the personal cost. There is, however, a second way of responding to the question. Rather than conceiving of Christ as separate from us, we can see ourselves as participating in Christ's life. Then we can see our intention to persevere and Christ's perseverance as not distinct but related realities. Since "All that Christ is, he gives to us" and "All that Christ has, he shares with us", Christ's perseverance is, in truth, ours.[31] His perseverance has been given to us by grace; we receive it in faith but we have to realize it in our lives, by learning to persevere through Christ's courage and strength. Paul, in his first letter to the church in Corinth, reminds his brothers and sisters that God has given them Christ's life. "He is the source of your life in Christ Jesus, who became for us wisdom from God, and righteousness and sanctification and redemption, in order that, as it is written, 'Let the one who boasts, boast in the Lord'" (1 Corinthians 1:30–1).

Knowing Christ in his death and resurrection

At the Last Supper, Jesus' teaching on his death, and how his disciples need to identify themselves with his cross and by his cross, reaches its climax. He tells them that they must eat his body and drink his cup. Thereby, his death is in them, and they are in his death. Only through his death can they experience his risen life. This dying and rising, their immersion in his death and resurrection, is to be the distinctive feature of their life together and the defining marker of their discipleship. Eating the symbols of Jesus' death, his body and blood, is a fulfilment of our baptism. Baptism is the rite of entry into God's Church and consuming Christ's body and blood are markers of belonging: eating from the one loaf is fundamental to belonging to Christ and his Church (1 Corinthians 10:17). In the Eucharist, through penitence, our heeding of the Word of God, and our intercessory prayer for the Church and world, we are led to the point of encountering Christ who has become our food and drink. Through the liturgy, we are prepared to respond to God's invitation to meet Christ and share God's life through the bread we eat and the wine we drink.

George Herbert, priest and poet in the seventeenth century, captures the wonder of grace in this encounter with Christ in his famous poem "Love III":

> Love bade me welcome; yet my soul drew back,
> Guilty of dust and sin.
> But quick-eyed Love, observing me grow slack from my
> entrance in,
> Drew nearer to me, sweetly questioning
> If I lack'd anything.
>
> 'A guest,' I answer'd, 'worthy to be here.'
> Love said, 'You shall be he.'
> 'I, the unkind, ungrateful? Ah, my dear,
> I cannot look on Thee.'
> Love took my hand, and smiling did reply,
> 'Who made the eyes but I?'
>
> 'Truth, Lord, but I have marr'd them: let my shame
> Go where it doth deserve.'
> 'And know you not,' says Love, 'Who bore the blame?'
> 'My dear, then I will serve.'
> 'You must sit down,' says Love, 'and taste my meat.'
> So I did sit and eat.[32]

Having met Christ in the Eucharist, we see Christ everywhere and in everyone

Having tasted and seen God's love in Christ in the Eucharist, we enter more fully into Christ's life. We learn to live eucharistically, sharing in Christ's constant gratitude to the Father. We see how God's love embraces the whole of life and enfolds everyone; we experience life more intensely and sense that the world is the sacrament of Christ's presence. We gradually become open to meeting Christ everywhere and through everyone.

Thomas Merton was an American monk, writer, theologian, mystic, poet, social activist and scholar of comparative religion in the twentieth century. In his book *Confessions of a Guilty Bystander*, he relates a profound experience of the glory of God and God's all-encompassing love in Louisville in the USA:

> In Louisville, at the corner of Fourth and Walnut, in the centre of the shopping district, I was suddenly overwhelmed with the realization that I loved all those people, that they were mine and I theirs, that we could not be alien to one another even though we were total strangers. It was like waking from a dream of separateness, of spurious self-isolation in a special world, the world of renunciation and supposed holiness ... This sense of liberation from an illusory difference was such a relief and such a joy to me that I almost laughed out loud ... I have the immense joy of being man, a member of a race in which God Himself became incarnate. As if the sorrows and stupidities of the human condition could overwhelm me, now I realize what we all are. And if only everybody could realize this! But it cannot be explained. There is no way of telling people that they are all walking around shining like the sun. Then it was as if I suddenly saw the secret beauty of their hearts, the depths of their hearts, where neither sin nor desire nor self-knowledge can reach, the core of their reality, the person that each one is in God's eyes. If only they could all see themselves as they really are. If only we could see each other that way all the time.[33]

Prayer

Crucified and Risen Christ, we long to know you. Help us to see you in the faces of those around us, in the world about us, and through the care of friend and stranger. Amen.

CHAPTER 8

Looking for the coming of the kingdom

And the one who was seated on the throne said,
"See, I am making all things new."
Revelation 21:5

I officiated one summer at a wedding blessing in Italy at an indisputably romantic location featured on a TV programme called *First Date*. The hotel and chapel were perched at the top of a hill, set in olive groves, with mountains as a backdrop and a sweeping landscape to the front. The views whichever way you looked were breathtaking. After an emotional service with lots of tears and laughter, there was a traditional wedding breakfast with multiple courses of delicious Italian cuisine. With the couple centre stage, we continued to celebrate their love, which had brought over eighty people together from the UK for a few days.

Over the festivities, the families and friends melded together. The husband and wife spoke movingly of how thankful they were that they had found each other, fallen in love, and were here in this wonderful setting, surrounded by so many of the people they loved. Gifts, hugs and kisses signalled new relationships formed or old ones renewed. Delicious food continued to be served and plenty of wine flowed as we moved from a formal dinner to an evening buffet and then onto a pool-side disco. As I joked with my colleagues, this was one of my tougher ministerial assignments! Celebrating the couple's love and faith, and enjoying each other's company in a beautiful location, I thought of how Jesus often compared the kingdom of God to a great party. As well as the honour of blessing their marriage and appreciating the whole event immensely, I felt that we had enjoyed something special, a foretaste of the kingdom of God.

Feasting in the kingdom of God

In the Eucharist, we follow Christ through death, resurrection and ascension. We journey with him into the kingdom of God; there we revel in the heavenly banquet in the Father's presence and we eat and drink at his table (Luke 22:30). Feasting is the primary metaphor for the abundance of life that God longs to give us in creation and at the End (Genesis 1:29; Luke 22:30). At the Last Supper, Jesus speaks of the wine that will flow when the kingdom of God comes, and earth and heaven are joined under the reign of God. Having ascended in triumph, uniting heaven and earth in the kingdom of God, Christ is glorified and reigns with the Father and the Holy Spirit. He invites us to enjoy the delights of the divine banquet and celebrate God's goodness and grace, now and in eternity.

If we understand Jesus' final meal with his disciples as a Passover meal, the cup after the supper is the "cup of blessing," the third of the Passover cups. Jesus blesses and drinks from that third cup, and leaves before drinking the fourth, traditionally associated with the coming kingdom, the new age, saying, "I tell you, I will never again drink of the fruit of the vine until that day when I drink it new with you in my Father's kingdom" (Matthew 26:29). Through Jesus, we experience the kingdom in our lives now but we await its consummation when heaven and earth are joined at the End. In the meantime, we pray "Thy kingdom come", and thirst for the justice and peace of God's kingdom (Matthew 26:29).

In the Eucharist, we anticipate the fulfilment of God's intention for creation and the coming of God's kingdom.[34] Confident that the kingdom of God is coming, the Church is an eschatological community, eagerly waiting for the climactic celebration of Christ's victory (Revelation 19:7–9).

The Church's life flows from the Eucharist. Outside of our worship together, our shared life is marked by work and rest, recreation and mealtimes. While there are periods of time in the life of the Church set aside for fasting, when we may literally abstain from food or metaphorically fast through other acts of self-denial, our life together is chiefly defined by feasting. Toward the end of my curacy, I was looking through the parish profiles aimed at prospective vicars. I handed one to my training incumbent and asked him what he thought. His first observation was that "they need to learn to party". He had detected in their description of the church's life an earnest quality, and he sensed that they needed to relax, enjoy each other's company more and take themselves less seriously. While God's work deserves our best, we can develop an unhealthy intensity which is more about our anxiety than our dedication. In amongst the demands and difficulties, there needs to be laughter and celebration too. There must be times of partying and the occasional feast. Feasting is marked by relaxation, a break from the effort of work; it is an expression of love, joy and generosity. We are to rejoice!

Time, eternity, and the kingdom of God

As we wait for the coming of the kingdom of God, we are between morning and evening, between Sunday and Sunday, between the two comings of Christ. Each Eucharist is a fulfilment of time itself because we experience the joy of participation in the kingdom. Sharing in the glorious resurrection of Christ, we know the unique and truly eschatological experience of joy, the fragrance of the Holy Spirit. Between Eucharists, we live in this in-between time, enjoying Christ's presence but looking forward to being together again. We eagerly anticipate the next time we will celebrate the Eucharist and know the joy of the resurrection in our midst. Our experience of the End in the Eucharist heightens our desire for the coming of the kingdom and our longing to see Jesus face to face.

I heard Tony Campolo, the American sociologist and pastor, preach a brilliant sermon, punctuated by the refrain, "It's Friday but Sunday is coming". Taking his listeners back to the crucifixion, he cited all that might depress people about their lives and the world. He reminded them that they were not to be surprised by these hard experiences; after all, he said, "It's Friday". Each time, he moved on to the Christian hope, grounded in the resurrection of Christ which was first hailed on a Sunday morning. He urged his listeners not to despair but to remember that "Sunday's coming". For us, Sunday represents resurrection, the coming of the kingdom at the End, and the next time we are to celebrate the Eucharist. When life is tough for us, we can echo his refrain, "It's Friday but Sunday's coming." Whenever we suffer, we can know Christ's death, and as we share Christ's death, we know that resurrection is coming. This is the hope that sustains us when we grieve for a loved one, a lost future, a role that has finished, a friendship that has ended.

We must also remember, however, that in God's economy, nothing is ever wasted, and all time is redeemed. "All, in the end, is harvest," as Edith Sitwell, a twentieth-century poet, so elegantly put it.[35] In the incarnation, eternity has entered the temporal succession of events; time participates through Christ in eternity. This means that Christ brings our past and our future into the present to heal our wounds, and to lift our eyes to the coming of the kingdom. In Christ, every day resounds with his victorious affirmation: "Behold, I make all things new." Through his renewing presence, our lives can become the sacrament of the world to come, shot through with the love and grace of the kingdom of God (Revelation 21:5–6).

At the End, the Holy Spirit will permeate and pervade creation. In the transformation of the people and the bread and wine in the Eucharist, this consummation of God's purposes for creation is prefigured. In the Eucharist, we anticipate the coming of Christ's universal kingdom when the whole created order will glorify God. Then, we will sit down to eat with our forerunners in the faith at the great banquet of heaven and enjoy God's welcome (Matthew 8:11). We can imagine our named place at the table for as Jesus said, "I go and prepare a place for you" (John 14:3). The picture of the great feast in the New Age was integral to Jesus' preaching of the kingdom. This image is drawn from the great prophets of the Old Testament, who see the age of the Messiah in terms of unlimited supplies of food and drink.[36] Feasting means joy, and joy is the spring and source of the Christian life, and the goal to which we are orientated.

Christ is at the centre of creation and is the Coming One

To recognize that Christ is the heart of creation is to be open to the joy of his presence in everyday life. The Christ who is at the centre of existence, who holds everything and everyone in being, is the Christ who preached and healed in Galilee and was crucified. He is made known to us through the proclamation, founded on the Scriptures, of the crucified and risen Jesus. As he can be encountered too in our everyday experience, we look forward to meeting Christ in the people we meet and in the goodness of the world around us.

The Bible tells us that we can particularly know Christ's presence in and through those on the edge: people we serve at the food bank; those we visit in prison; parents crippled by debt who cannot afford to buy clothes for their children; in the asylum seeker and refugee, and those we see on our screens dying of thirst because of a drought. Whatever we do for them, we do for Christ (Matthew 25:31–46).

The Christ who is proclaimed through the Scriptures is also the Coming One. In the encounter with Cleopas and his companion on the Emmaus road, as soon as Christ is identified by them, he disappears (Luke 24:13–35). While the Church knows Christ through the Holy Spirit, the Church is also aware of his absence. We know him now intimately but long to see him face-to-face. The Church is waiting for the return of Christ in glory to fulfil finally God's purposes for creation. Therefore, Christians are oriented towards the future—towards the Christ who is coming (Philippians 3:20–1, Revelation 22:17). Our longing for the coming of Christ in his kingdom is strengthened by our experience of Christ in the Eucharist. Our thirst is eased, yet not quenched. Our hunger is abated, but not sated. Though aware of his presence, we yearn to see him.

As we wait for his final coming, we prepare to see him face-to-face by continuing along the path of holiness. Our complete being—body, mind and heart—is brought into a new unity, as we learn to cooperate with the Holy Spirit. During this ongoing, steady conversion of life, we learn through prayer and patience to participate in Christ's reconciling ministry. Thereby, we help our contemporaries to welcome Christ, into their lives now and when he comes in glory.

While we wait for the Coming One, we keep our eyes fixed on him: "Therefore, since we are surrounded by so great a cloud of witnesses, let us also lay aside every weight and the sin that clings so closely, and let us run with perseverance the race that is set before us, looking to Jesus the pioneer and perfecter of our faith, who for the sake of the joy that was set before him endured the cross, disregarding its shame, and has taken his seat at the right hand of the throne of God" (Hebrews 12:1–2).

Prayer

Almighty and everlasting God,
increase in us your gift of faith
that, forsaking what lies behind
and reaching out to that which is before,
we may run the way of your commandments
and win the crown of everlasting joy;
through Jesus Christ your Son our Lord,
who is alive and reigns with you,
in the unity of the Holy Spirit,
one God, now and for ever. Amen.[37]

Part 2

The rest of the book is a journey through the liturgy of the Eucharist, drawing upon *Common Worship*, one of the two authorized Church of England books of services and prayers.

CHAPTER 9

Gathering

We have come together in the name of the Father, Son and Holy Spirit.[38]

It is Sunday morning and Carol is loath to get out of bed to go to church. Her mum, Sue, calls up the stairs, "Are you up yet? It's 9 a.m. and the service begins in an hour." "I don't want to go," Carol responds, and rolls over and pulls the duvet over her head. Sue shouts back, "You've got to go." Fifteen minutes later with no sound of movement upstairs, Sue chivvies her again, "I hope that you're out of bed." Carol calls back defiantly, "I don't want to go. The choir is tuneless and the sermons tedious." Sue, with greater vehemence this time, simply replies, "You've got to go." When it gets to 9.30 a.m. and there is still no sign of Carol, Sue tries again, this time plaintively, "Look Carol, in fifteen minutes, we must leave, otherwise we'll be late. I hope that you're almost ready." Carol remains adamant "Look, I am fed up with church. The service is so boring." Sue's riposte is to the point, "Carol, no more nonsense. You've not got a choice; you're the organist."

The Church—a people called to gather

This story reminds us of how everyone in church on a Sunday morning has got ready and travelled to be there. Let us hope that most people come with a great deal more enthusiasm than Carol the organist! As we prepare to come to church, it is good to remember all those doing likewise from different locations and varying home situations. Everyone sitting around us in church has gone through the same routine: all of them have got up, left home, travelled to church, arrived, been welcomed and sat down. Simultaneously, but separately, we have all been brought together. This sense of being gathered underlies the original meaning of the word "church" as a people called out by God to be "a chosen race, a royal priesthood, a holy nation, God's own people" proclaiming God's "mighty acts" in a particular place (1 Peter 2:9). Formed into a community by God, we gather on a Sunday, drawn by the crucified Christ who declared, "I, when I am lifted up from the earth, will draw all people to myself" (John 12:32).

Before we set out or on the way, we can pray for each other that when we arrive in church, we will be ready to give and receive from God. Those with certain responsibilities—the person leading the service, the preacher, the musicians, those reading the Bible, those welcoming, whoever is leading our prayers of intercession, to name some—can be a specific focus in our prayers before the service. In our waiting for the service to begin, we could look around and pray for those we sense are struggling. A look of sadness in someone's eyes, or drooped shoulders, or a tired face, can prompt us to pray for that individual, and that all those who are feeling low may be lifted and strengthened. By these prayers, we open ourselves and those for whom we pray to the Holy Spirit, who draws us all closer together and to God.

Churches are sacred spaces, set aside for God's people to meet with God. As places where we come expecting to encounter God, they are special, regardless of their scale or grandeur. Our attitude to the place where we gather to worship God, whether it is a school hall, a community centre, a marquee in a park, or a church, is to be the same as Jacob's to the location he named Bethel, "the house of God" (Genesis 28:17). Jacob is fleeing his older brother Esau, who is furious with him because he has taken their father's blessing, which was by right the prerogative of the first-born son. At the end of a day's journeying, Jacob settles down to sleep in a "certain place," and sees in his dream, "a ladder set up on the earth, the top of it reaching to heaven; and the angels of God were ascending and descending on it". Then God speaks to him, affirming that Jacob has been chosen to fulfil the promise made to Abraham that through him "all the families of the earth shall be blessed". When Jacob awakes, he declares, "How awesome is this place! This is none other than the house of God, and this is the gate of heaven" (Genesis 28:10–22).

When we come to the place where we are to celebrate the Eucharist, we echo in our hearts Jacob's insight, "This is none other than the house of God; this is the gate of heaven."

Gathering to encounter God

A leader of a university mission told of how he had been given the theme of the week. When praying, he had seen himself walking through St James's Park in London on a sunny afternoon. He noticed an impressive figure sitting on a bench, and somehow, he knew that it was God. When their eyes met, God called out his name, and beckoned him to come over. As he approached, God moved to one side to create space for him. He sat down and God duly offered him a sandwich, cheese and tomato, his favourite, and a bottle of water. As they ate and drank, the conversation flowed and he found himself telling God about his life, his hopes and fears. After talking together for some time, they sat in a contented silence for a while. When he looked at his watch, he could not believe how late it was. He explained to God that he needed to go, thanked God and headed home, feeling buoyed up and affirmed by their meeting. When the vision was over, he knew what was to be the central focus of his talks. He spoke powerfully on each of the seven nights of the mission of how "God wants our company". Besides serving as a summary of the Christian Gospel, "God wants our company" could feature on invitations and publicity about church services. Whenever we assemble for worship, we are responding to God's invitation to enjoy God's hospitality. We therefore come together "in the name of the Father, Son and Holy Spirit".

While God wants our company, God also desires everyone else's company too. As Jesus exemplified, God's love encompasses all, even those regarded by others as unlikely recipients. The way he related to outcasts—prostitutes, tax collectors, lepers and lawbreakers—challenged prevailing attitudes. He urged a different approach: the disreputable should not be shunned but welcomed; the weak must not be rebuffed but embraced.

Following his baptism and the launch of his public ministry, Jesus soon became notorious for keeping the wrong sort of company. For those with whom he ate and drank, the experience was transformative. Luke in his Gospel tells us the story of Zacchaeus, a tax collector. Working for the Roman oppressors and overcharging to line his own pockets, he was spurned by the people of his town, Jericho. Hearing that Jesus—the charismatic wonderworker from Galilee—is approaching, Zacchaeus goes to see, but being both late and short, he is forced to clamber up a tree to see over the heads of the crowd. When Jesus draws level with where Zacchaeus is perched up in the tree, he stops and calls him by name to come down. Jesus tells him that he wants to spend time with him, to enjoy his hospitality, and they go to his home. Eating and drinking with Jesus opens up Zacchaeus to God and his neighbour, and he is radically changed. He goes to the public square in Jericho and announces to the astonished crowd that he is going to give away half of his possessions to the poor and pay back those he has cheated four times what he took from them. In response to Zacchaeus' conversion, Jesus said, "Today salvation has come to this house, because he too is a son of Abraham. For the Son of Man came to seek out and to save the lost" (Luke 19:9–10). Jesus sets Zacchaeus free. Secure in God's love, Zacchaeus no longer needs to cling on to his wealth. He can let go, and be transformed by the love and life of God. Through Jesus, those who are lost are found and those who are dead are given life.

After Jesus has been raised from the dead, the disciples, who had betrayed him and deserted him, experience God's grace in even greater measure. Jesus meets with those disciples who have returned to Galilee to fish and shares a meal with them (John 21). Despite their denial and desertion of Jesus at the cross, he offers them a breakfast of fish and bread without rancour or reprimand. He is the welcoming host, and hospitality is offered and enjoyed.

When Peter tells Cornelius, a Roman centurion, and his relatives and his friends about Jesus, he describes how the disciples "ate and drank with him after he rose from the dead" (Acts 10:41). Post-resurrection, Jesus is still the one who eats and drinks with his friends. "Those who eat and drink with Jesus" is a simple definition of God's Church. We come together to eat bread and drink wine in the Eucharist as guests, invited and welcomed by Jesus. Our company is longed for and desired; we are loved and cherished. Those who gather together around Jesus come from different family backgrounds, and represent diverse cultures and nationalities, yet are united by him.

When we meet together, we serve and pray for one another, and are caught up in a great exchange of giving and receiving. Focused on Jesus, we become receptive to God's transforming love. In God's presence, we are penitent, yet full of praise: we are dust, yet are created to glorify God. By encountering God, we realize anew our own frailty and our own destiny for we are becoming more Christlike, and when we meet him, "we will be like him" (1 John 3:2).

Gathering for worship

The Latin maxim *Lex orandi, lex credendi, lex vivendi* states the truth that how we pray determines what we believe and how we live. The liturgy of the Eucharist carries and conveys the Christian understanding of the world, and our responsibilities within it. By praying it we are given the power to be disciples, serving each other and God. The Eucharist expresses too our utter dependence on God and, in response to God's unwavering faithfulness, we give thanks. As we pray the liturgy, we serve God—this is work we are given to do—and pray on behalf of the world. In this joyful task, we need to be energized by the Holy Spirit, as we do in every facet of Christian discipleship, to participate in Christ's eternal self-offering to the Father and to join with the "angels and archangels, and with all the company of heaven" in the eternal worship of heaven.[39]

Gathering to journey together

On a Christian nurture course, I was leading a session on the Eucharist, and one of the candidates, relatively new to faith, was trying to explain how she had found her first experience of this act of worship. Stammering and searching for the right words to express what was clearly a powerful experience for her, she hit on this wonderful insight: "It's like entering a different world." I agree.

In the Eucharist, we enter into God's kingdom, signified by the singing of heaven's endless hymn of praise, the Sanctus: "Holy, holy, holy Lord, God of power and might, heaven and earth are full of your glory. Hosanna in the highest".[40] We are indeed in a "different world", the world to come, united and perfected in Christ (Ephesians 1:8–10). As the Church enters eternity in the Eucharist, we see the goal of the Church's mission: the hallowing of the created order and the restoration of all things in Christ. We return to the world to bear witness to this reality.

Gathering to feast together

In *Babette's Feast* by Karen Blixen, Babette arrives in a remote Danish village as a refugee from armed conflict in Paris. She offers to work for free for two elderly and pious sisters, Martine and Philippa, whose father was the pastor of a strict and dour Protestant sect. Her only link with her past life in Paris is a friend who buys for her a lottery ticket each year. In the fourteenth year of her stay, Babette wins the lottery and receives the sizeable sum of 10,000 francs. She proposes to Martine and Philippa that she gives a lavish dinner for them, and the ageing and depleted congregation of the dutiful sect. Babette buys a wonderful array of ingredients and cooks a sumptuous dinner. Initially, the twelve guests are wary of each other and uneasy about how much money has been spent. However, with each successive course and as the wine flows, conversation becomes more animated and tension dissipates. The delicious food and fine wine make everyone feel special, and they are united in their sense of privilege. After all, they have done nothing to deserve such a spectacular evening. The mood soon becomes jovial, and the exchanges swing between the humorous and the serious, but everyone is learning to be authentic, real with each other. In the resulting bonhomie, old wrongs are forgiven and forgotten, love is rekindled and over the table settles a mysterious sense of renewal.

Against the contemporary obsession with targets in public services, business, and even in the Church of England, along with the frequent requirement to carry out a "cost and benefit analysis" before we embark on any new venture, a feast seems particularly extravagant, even reckless.

Still, the short story of *Babette's Feast* reminds us of the importance and power of celebrations.

Gathering as the Church

We come together at God's invitation, to relish God's hospitality and to share God's love. What we experience when we are gathered, we offer to others when we are dispersed. As we come together in the name of the Father, Son and Holy Spirit, we go to live in the name of the triune God.

We are the recipients of God's grace, mercy and peace because of God's love for us. Since God's love embraces everyone, God urges us to share what we have received so that all may know God's goodness and grace. If we seek to hold on to God's gifts for ourselves, we restrict the flow of God's abundant love and restrain the scope of God's embrace. When we withhold from others what God has given us, we also jeopardize our own experience of God's grace and risk facing God's judgement. This is the truth behind the reciprocity of forgiveness in the Lord's Prayer: "Forgive us our sins, as we forgive those who sin against us." The forgiveness we receive from God must be offered to those who offend us. Similarly, in the parable of the unforgiving servant, the torment of the servant who refuses to cede a small debt to another servant, despite having had his large debt to the king cancelled, underlines Jesus' injunction to "forgive your brother or sister from your heart" (Matthew 18:23–35). Likewise, the parable that Jesus tells to his host, a Pharisee, to explain the actions of the woman who had interrupted their conversation to wash his feet with her tears and to wipe his feet with her hair, makes the same point: when we know how much we have been forgiven by God, there is an obligation on us to forgive each other (Luke 7:36–50). How God is towards us, we are to be towards each other. As God is forgiving to us, we are to forgive. In the same way that God is merciful to us, we need to be merciful. As God loves us generously, we are to love generously too.

Gathering in the name of Jesus

Christians are defined as those who, inspired by the Holy Spirit, "call on the name of our Lord Jesus Christ" (1 Corinthians 1:2; 12:3). The name of Jesus is both intimate, "For, 'Everyone who calls upon the name of the Lord shall be saved,'" and also awesome, "At the name of Jesus every knee should bend, in heaven and on earth and under the earth, and every tongue should confess that Jesus Christ is Lord, to the glory of God the Father" (Romans 10:13; Philippians 2:10–11). By faith in the name of Jesus, we gather to open ourselves to God's presence and to the saving power of the Holy Trinity in our midst.

Prayer

> Gather us in and hold us forever
> Gather us in and make us your own
> Gather us in, all peoples together
> Fire of love in our flesh and our bones.[41]

CHAPTER 10

Purity of heart

Blessed are the pure in heart, for they will see God.
Matthew 5:8

One of my friends who has been a Christian for many years tells how, on one Sunday, a familiar prayer gave her a deeper awareness of God's love.

"I have often envied those who have had a dramatic 'conversion' experience; I was brought up in a Christian home, baptized as a baby and confirmed in my teens. In the parable of the Waiting Father, I quite often find myself identifying with the Elder Brother, rather than the Prodigal Son, wishing that I could have had his powerful experience of return and welcome. There have, however, been some significant moments in my spiritual journey which have deepened my faith and made it more real. In my teens and early twenties, I was very pious, went regularly to confession and church, and felt that if I took my 'best bits' to God in prayer and kept to the rules, he would accept me. Suddenly one day in the Eucharist the prayer known as the *Collect for Purity* really hit me. The beginning of the prayer undid me. This time when I prayed, "Almighty God, to whom all hearts are open, all desires known, and from whom no secrets are hidden", I realized that I could not kid God—he knew me better than I knew myself: my shortcomings, my struggles, my pain—and though it was really hard for me to accept, I knew that God loved me in all my mess. This realization, that it was pointless to be anything less than fully honest with God, changed my prayer life immediately."[42]

Getting ready to worship

In preparation for the Eucharist, we can turn to God and call upon the Holy Spirit to prepare us to participate fully in heart and mind in our worship of God. We might also, even if only occasionally, enrich our engagement with the service through one or more of these practices: we can take a look at one or more of the Bible passages that will feature in the service; we can spend some time reflecting on our lives; we can determine to pray for someone or something in particular; and we can mull over the preceding week, and name what has been especially good and a cause for gratitude.

When it comes to exploring one or more of the biblical texts to be read in our worship, identifying the genre of the passage is a good starting point. Is the passage a poem, a parable, or myth, history or part of a letter to a church or individual, or from a Gospel or drawn from a prophetic book? We might also consider what precedes and follows the set text, and how it fits into the overall themes of the particular book, and the Bible as a whole. If any word or verse puzzles us, we can find out more through a Bible commentary or in conversation with someone who might know more than we do. This prior engagement with these texts will help us to be more alert to what God is saying to us through them when we hear them read and expounded in the sermon.

We can also spend some time in personal reflection. This helps to integrate what we experience in worship into the rest of our lives. We could use the Beatitudes or the two great commandments as a reference point (Matthew 5:1–11; Mark 12:28–33). By holding before ourselves the markers of discipleship and recalling God's high aspiration that we learn to love as God loves, we can consider how we are faring, see when have not done so well, and sense where we are seeing the fruit of our faith, in our own lives and the lives of others.

In our reflection on our lives, we are aware that we are living in an increasingly narcissistic culture. Pervasive advertising that pops up everywhere encourages us to spend more and more money on ourselves because we are "worth it".[43] It feeds a "me-first" culture, where my desires trump any sense of collective responsibility. We need to be wary that we are not sucked into this competitive mentality, which is the antithesis of the Christian emphasis on loving and serving others. We are to pay attention to Paul's command to the church in Rome, "Do not be conformed to this world, but be transformed by the renewing of your minds, so that you may discern what is the will of God—what is good and acceptable and perfect" (Romans 12:2).

The self-forgetful humility we seek can only be found indirectly, by concentrating on loving God and loving people; striving to be humble is self-defeating. (A self-conscious quest to be humble is bound to lead to its opposite, pride, or despair.) As we examine our lives, and how we have lived in the preceding week in particular, we remember Christ's example and grace. He is committed to teaching us how best to serve others, and to bear our responsibility for our neighbour and for creation. We come to the Eucharist ready to cast in the fire of God's love whatever hinders our discipleship and delays our growth in holiness. We come to celebrate God's work so far in our lives and God's promise to transform us into the likeness of Christ. We come to offer ourselves to God.

We can also identify a specific focus for our prayers. We remember those we are always holding in our hearts, especially our family and friends. We consider our church and our locality, and the wider world. We ask God if there is someone or some situation that God is asking us to offer in prayer in our worship. We could look back over recent days and recognize God's faithfulness woven into the fabric of our lives. We can also pinpoint specific gifts that we have especially appreciated, and come ready to add our voice to the chorus of thanksgiving. We are to come with grateful hearts.

The path to holiness

Christ calls us to grow in holiness. As we journey along this path that demands dedication and discipline, we discover a greater detachment—a freedom from all that would agitate the spirit—and a developing trust—a childlike confidence in God.

We set ourselves free from the sway of our emotions and the swirl of our thoughts by paying attention to our internal life. If we are distracted most of the time, we are likely to find being focused in prayer more difficult. Brother Lawrence, a lay brother in a Carmelite monastery in Paris in the seventeenth century, wrote in his eighth letter: "... you should keep the mind strictly in the presence of God, and being accustomed to thinking of God often, you will find it easy to keep your mind calm at the time of prayer or at least recall it from 'wanderings.'"[44] When we notice our thoughts following strange paths or going down a dead end, we can offer these wanderings simply to Christ and return to the task in hand. We are to try to be fixed on whatever God has given us to do whether that is listening to someone, chairing a meeting or writing an email. This can, of course, be difficult, especially if we are tired or troubled by anxious thoughts. Yet, we aim to give our work, the individual we are facing, or the prayer we are offering our full attention. Punctuating the day with short prayers, such as the Jesus Prayer, "Lord Jesus Christ, Son of God, have mercy upon me, a sinner", or a verse from the Psalms, such as, "I give you thanks, O Lord, with my whole heart", can help us to stay attentive to God and what God is asking us to do (Psalm 138:1).

As we learn to turn to Christ with greater frequency during each day, the Holy Spirit refines our thoughts and moulds our hearts. This purification of the heart bears fruit in our relationship with other people—we are less likely to try to possess or impress—and leads to a greater intimacy with God: "Blessed are the pure in heart, for they will see God" (Matthew 5:8). As we draw closer to God, we see ourselves with greater clarity in the light of God's truth.

Self-knowledge, as all mystics insist, is integral to holiness. Therefore, we need to be honest before God. There is no point pretending because God knows us better than we know ourselves. Liberated by God's love, we are free to offer ourselves to God with our strengths and weaknesses; there is nothing we can do to make God love us more or to love us less. As we know ourselves better, we are better placed to give who we are to God. Who we think we are and who we actually are become more closely aligned as our relationship with God deepens, so we become profoundly aware of God's love for us as we truly are. We know too that we are a "work in progress", and that by God's compassionate shaping of our lives, we are steadily becoming more ourselves, the person we were created to be. Assured of God's faithful and generous love, we slowly abandon all pretence, and each of us learns to rest "just as I am" in God's love.[45]

Prayer

Almighty God,
to whom all hearts are open,
all desires known,
and from whom no secrets are hidden:
cleanse the thoughts of our hearts
by the inspiration of your Holy Spirit,
that we may perfectly love you,
and worthily magnify your holy name;
through Christ our Lord.
Amen.[46]

CHAPTER 11

Penitence

Love so amazing, so divine, demands my soul, my life, my all.[47]

John and Dave had met on their first day of infant school and had been friends ever since. Now in their late teens and both West Ham supporters, they went to every home game together. Afterwards, they would head to a nearby pub either to drown their sorrows or celebrate victory, or to decide, in the event of a draw, whether they should be disappointed or content. On one occasion, they moved on from chatting about football to talking about their friendship, and concluded that they were "really good mates". Then John teased Dave about the depth of their friendship, "Dave, if you had a million pounds, you'd give me half, wouldn't you?" "Of course, I would," Dave replied. John continued, "What about if you had one hundred thousand pounds?" "Sure thing," Dave assured John. John tested Dave further, "What about if you had one hundred pounds?" Dave, this time was indignant. "Now that's not fair, John, you know that I've got a hundred pounds in my wallet." They both laughed uproariously. Behind the humour of this exchange is a serious point: whereas hypothetical generosity is easy, actually being generous is costly. This, though, is the test of the depth of our love: it is seen in how much it costs us. That is why we see the depth of God's love supremely in the cross of Christ.

The cross—confession, forgiveness and renewal

Whereas the cross serves God's loving purposes for humanity, it is on a human level a tragedy. An innocent man has been unjustly sentenced and brutally killed. The Messiah, God's Son, is outrageously executed. We cannot, though, distance ourselves from the perpetrators of this scandal. While those who conspired against Jesus must take direct responsibility for his death, they also represent humanity, albeit at its worst. Behind their plotting lies the dark desires that lodge in the human heart. We can blame them, but we are implicated. They are guilty, yet we are not innocent.

There is, then, a collective responsibility: we are all complicit in Jesus' rejection and crucifixion. His body nailed to the cross bears witness to the depths of humanity's alienation from God. The crucifixion of God's Christ brings into sharp focus the world's opposition to God. This is humanity's calamity and our desolation. We may want to point the finger and proclaim our innocence, but there is no shying away from the harsh reality: our self-seeking has been starkly revealed for all to see. In the tortured frame of Jesus, our sin is laid bare; we are undone and judged by the cross.

As the plot to have Jesus killed gathered pace, humanity's pursuit of self-interest fired up the protagonists. When Pontius Pilate, the Roman governor, ordered that Jesus be crucified, he put political expediency ahead of what was just. Jesus, by his constant refusal to collude and his robust goodness, discloses in his antagonists the murky recesses of the human heart. We hear, in the cry of Jesus on the cross, humanity's alienation from God: "My God, my God, why have you forsaken me?" We sometimes feel forsaken because we have chosen to abandon God; never because God has abandoned us.

The choice to live independently of God, our preference to assert ourselves over and against God, is the "original sin", the one from which all others flow. When we search for meaning without reference to God, we are under the delusion that we are self-sufficient, that we do not need God. The cross makes it clear that this quest is forlorn and futile; it is a cul-de-sac, a dead end. Sin leads to death: Jesus' death underlines this truth and undermines our self-satisfaction (Romans 6:23). By killing

Christ, humanity embraces death, for to reject Christ is to turn our backs on life. Paradoxically, the cross is also the symbol of God's mercy, the guarantee of our forgiveness. In Christ's death, we are restored to life, and reconciled to God.

Whereas the cross is humanity's decisive defeat, the cross is God's ultimate victory. Death is tasted by Christ and vanquished, evil unmasked and overcome, and God is victorious. As we gaze at the cross, we see both the "horror and darkness of our plight" and the "glory of divine grace".[48] The light of God cannot be quenched, and illuminates the way to the kingdom of love that has become our destiny. Christ has broken down the dividing wall of hostility, creating one humanity reconciled to God (Ephesians 2:13–16). In the words of Karl Barth, the famous twentieth-century Swiss theologian, on the cross, the "Judge is judged in our place"—our salvation is secured, and the whole of humanity and creation drawn into a unity.

At the cross, Christ unites humanity and the entire created order in his self-giving to the Father. As Christ gives his life on the cross, the Father, in the power of the Holy Spirit, is reconciling the world to himself (2 Corinthians 5:18–19; Romans 6:23). The Church, representing humanity, bears witness to God's forgiveness, which gives us the joy of the "world to come".

Chastened by humanity's culpability for his death but celebrating our inclusion in Christ's self-offering on the cross, we stand in the grace of God, and are ready to acknowledge that we were at Calvary. Thus, we can respond, "Yes, we were there" to this spiritual's repeated question, "Were you there?"

> Were you there when they crucified my
>   Lord? Yes, we were there.
> Were you there when they nailed him to
>   the cross? Yes, we were there.
> Were you there when they pierced him in
>   the side? Yes, we were there.
> Were you there when the sun refused to
>   shine? Yes, we were there.

Confronted by the crucified Jesus, we know that we cannot deny our responsibility for his betrayal and death. Like the first disciples when they met with the Risen Christ, we know too that we are accepted and called to be companions of Christ—those who break bread with him—in a continuing journey. In meeting the Risen Christ, we know God's extraordinary forgiveness and compassion, and are renewed. Our prayers of penitence are our return to the "newness of life" which God gives to us "once and for all". Each time, we confess, we experience God's mercy, and are taken further into the self-offering of Christ to the Father that is defined for eternity by the cross.

Participating more fully in Christ's life requires us to step back from our own lives and re-orientate ourselves. Sometimes, instead of our reactions and actions stemming from our relationship with Christ, we behave unthinkingly. We let our emotions stir us up and dictate what we do. By pausing and being present to ourselves in those heated moments, we open ourselves up to God and learn to respond in the power of the Holy Spirit. Instead of stomping around and lashing out, we become people of peace. Leaving behind grumbling and grumpiness, we enjoy life more and find extra reasons to be thankful.

God's work of moulding us to be more like Jesus is unrelenting: God never gives up on us. Confident in God's faithfulness, we can be sure that when we see Christ face-to-face in eternity, we shall be like him (1 Corinthians 13:12). As Paul wrote, "I am confident of this, that the one who began a good work among you will bring it to completion by the day of Jesus Christ" (Philippians 1:6). In the prayers of penitence in the Eucharist, each one of us comes face-to-face with God. By acknowledging our sin, we are ready to receive forgiveness, know the purging fire of God's love, and be renewed. In our repentance—our turning away from sin and turning to Christ—we are given new life. Therefore, the purpose of confession is to receive forgiveness and renewal in the Holy Spirit. Using the simile of life being like travelling in a car, confession is like going to a petrol station, getting the car washed, filling up with fuel and then setting off again.

Our commission in baptism: to be a faithful servant to our life's end

At our baptism, we are commissioned to "fight valiantly against sin, the world and the devil". As we pray the confession, we admit that we sometimes lose the occasional battle: we can allow the power of sin to reassert its grip on us and act selfishly; the world with its temptations can draw us away from God, and evil can lead us to ignore or be caught up in wrongdoing. To confess is to recommit ourselves to God's work in our lives. As we turn to God in repentance, we assent to the work of the Holy Spirit in harmonizing our character and life with Christ's. This is the unceasing challenge and the enduring promise of Christian discipleship: God summons us and enables us to become more like Christ.

As we mature in our discipleship, we are more—not less, as one might think—aware of our need for renewal. Prayers of penitence are not to be a drastic remedy or an optional extra for the more passionate disciple but rather a habitual discipline, integral to the pursuit of holiness. Our penitence reminds us of the rigour of discipleship and our utter reliance on the help of the Holy Spirit. Only by hearing regularly Christ's call to follow him do we learn to walk in the way of Christian discipleship, the way of repentance and conversion of life, the way of the cross. Through the discipline of regular confession and the humility it fosters, we are changed "from one degree of glory to another . . . this comes from the Lord, the Spirit" (2 Corinthians 3:18).

Prayer

We adore you, Lord Jesus Christ, here and in all the churches throughout the world, and we bless you because by your holy cross, you have redeemed the world. Amen.[49]

CHAPTER 12

Praise and worship

Every day I will bless you, and praise your name for ever and ever. Great is the Lord, and greatly to be praised; his greatness is unsearchable.
Psalm 145:2–3

Jane was not sleeping. Daunted by the prospect of preaching for the first time, her nights were disturbed by dreams of losing her place or boring the congregation. Whenever she thought about getting up to preach and seeing the sea of faces looking back at her, she could feel her heart begin to race and a sick feeling in the pit of her stomach. Her anxiety spiralled upwards and out of control. The more she thought about it, the more fearful she became and the more it occupied her thoughts.

Jane turned to her longstanding friend, Sue, who reassured her that first-time nerves were normal; everybody in her shoes would be worried. As for her anxious thoughts, Sue proposed that they could be a spur to a growth in faith. Sue relayed how she too had been in the grip of fear at one stage in her life but had learnt, through her reading and the wise counsel of a friend, how to actively put her trust in God whenever she felt her anxiety mounting. She had discovered that a good way to turn to God in faith was through reciting biblical texts that spoke of God's strength and trusting God. Once the confidence in God expressed in these biblical verses had stilled her mind and encouraged her, Sue had found that then she would often want to praise God. Jane was grateful to Sue, and felt strengthened. She now had a way of combating her fears that would also help her grow in faith. Every time Jane became worried about the prospect of preaching, she would turn to the Bible. She found the psalms especially helpful and two verses in particular: "God is our refuge and strength, a very present help in trouble," and "O Most High, when I am afraid, I put my trust in you" (Psalm 46:1; Psalm 56:2–3). As she repeated these verses to herself, her faith deepened and, like Sue, she would end up praising God. That was how Jane learned to depend on God in the build-up to her initial sermon. When Jane got up to preach and saw those familiar faces smiling at her, she forgot herself and gave herself to the task at hand. Her first sermon met with acclaim but Jane, in characteristic fashion, deflected the praise to those who had helped and to God who once more had proved faithful. She had learned two important lessons about discipleship too: that trusting God is a choice, and one we need to make whenever we are afraid; and also that praise strengthens our confidence in God, both expressing and affirming our faith.

The Holy Spirit leads us from praise to an encounter with God

In the Eucharist, after we have confessed and been assured of God's forgiveness, we praise God, often singing or reciting the ancient words of the Gloria:

> Glory to God in the highest,
> and peace to his people on earth.
>
> Lord God, heavenly King,
> almighty God and Father,
> we worship you, we give you thanks,
> we praise you for your glory.
>
> Lord Jesus Christ, only Son of the Father,
> Lord God, Lamb of God,
> you take away the sin of the world:
> have mercy on us;
> you are seated at the right hand of the Father:
> receive our prayer.

> For you alone are the Holy One,
> you alone are the Lord,
> you alone are the Most High, Jesus Christ,
> with the Holy Spirit,
> in the glory of God the Father.
> Amen.[50]

The psalmist asks for God to open his mouth that God may be praised: "O Lord, open my lips, and my mouth will declare your praise" (Psalm 51:15). Praise is not produced by us unaided; we need the inspiration of the Spirit. The Holy Spirit reveals the truth about God to us, invites us into God's life, and, in response to God's goodness and grace, leads us to praise God.

Our praise of God transforms us. As we become more enthralled by God, our egos are displaced, forced to take a back seat. Over time, our focus shifts steadily on to God, and self-absorption gives way to rapt attention to God and God's agenda.

Praise is the prelude to an awareness of God's presence, a sense of encounter. What we affirm about God in praise becomes our direct experience of God; all we believe about God, we come to know for ourselves. What we express to God in praise, we know personally. Thereby, "I praise you for you are loving and faithful" becomes "I know you love me and are faithful to me."

Praise in the power of the Holy Spirit prepares us for God's mission

In the Eucharist, we are drawn into Christ, who leads us to the Father and into the kingdom. Having assumed our humanity in his incarnation, Christ leads us on this journey from death to resurrection and ascension. In the Father's presence in the kingdom of God, we know that we are God's children, and we rejoice in this exalted status conferred on us by God's grace in Christ. Here we understand the truth that our primary identity is that we are children of God.

As beloved children in the presence of God in the kingdom, we know that God longs for the whole of humanity to experience God's parental care. From this heavenly perspective, we can no longer be myopic, fixated on our own feelings and concerns, because we have the global view. We know that God is passionate about the welfare of everyone everywhere. We cannot ignore the world's gross disparities in wealth, the plight of refugees, those living in the middle of bloody conflicts, and those facing drought and hunger. Captivated as we are by God in worship, the test of the authenticity and depth of our encounter with God is seen in our subsequent engagement with the world. This intrinsic connection between our worship of God and God's mission to the whole created order is integral to the Eucharist. Through our prayers of intercession, we join in with Christ's prayer for the Church and for the world, and know his longing for justice and peace. When we stand in the Father's presence at the end of the Eucharistic Prayer, we are reminded again of the connection between heaven and earth: "Our Father . . . your kingdom come, your will be done on earth as it is in heaven." Christians have sometimes been accused of being so absorbed in religious practice that they are detached and careless about the world around them. People have been known to say, "They are so heavenly minded that they are of no earthly use." In truth, it is the opposite: it is when we are heavenly minded that we are of earthly use. Our vision of and longing for heaven drives us to seek justice and peace on earth. Loving God does not mean that we withdraw from the world but that we are passionately committed to the world.

Created to thank, praise, worship and adore God

In the central prayer of the service, the Eucharistic Prayer, the congregational response to the president's invitation to give thanks is, "It is right to give thanks and praise."[51] Thanks are given in response to what God has given; praise is offered because of who God is. Since God is good, loving and just, praise is due to God, everywhere and always. As our lives become typified by praise, we fulfil our human identity, for we are worshipping beings—*homo adorans*. This is the fundamental insight into the mystery of our humanity: we are made for worship. G. K. Chesterton, a writer and philosopher of the twentieth century, said that when people stop believing in God, they do not believe in nothing, they believe in anything. Similarly, when people stop worshipping God, they do not worship nothing, they worship anything. We do not have to look far to see the false gods that take up people's time and energy: money, power, sex and fame, to name a few.

In the Eucharist, we praise God for his faithfulness in creation. We experience God's goodness and love in creation in many different ways; for instance, in a sunrise; in a crunchy, juicy bite of an apple; in the love of a friend. Notwithstanding national and global catastrophes, such as earthquakes and pandemics, we still see and sense God's love through the world around us. We believe that the creation is essentially sacramental, a means of knowing and experiencing God's love. Creation's sacramentality is fulfilled by Jesus Christ. This human being mediates God's love in all he is and does. He is the embodiment of the Father's love. Through his life we experience God's love at every second of every day. This makes Jesus the ultimate and perfect sacrament; we know with unique clarity God's love through him.

Jesus confirms the goal of creation and humanity's purpose. Full of the Holy Spirit and living for God's glory, Jesus epitomizes the goal of the created order: creation suffused by the Holy Spirit to the glory of God. Jesus also fulfils humanity's purpose of relating lovingly to the Father. His life is continuous communion with the Father, interlaced with prayer and praise. By imitating Christ in praising God, we learn to offer our life back to the Father wholeheartedly. As we fill our days with thanks and praise, we fulfil our vocation as children of God by relating in love to the Father.

In the Eucharist, joining with the saints, angels and archangels, we participate in the praise and worship of heaven. In this act of worship, therefore, we prefigure the realization of the Christian vision of the End: humanity and the rest of the created order, and the whole company of heaven, worshipping God together. When God's loving purpose for creation is finally consummated, heaven and earth will be united in the inexpressible joy of praise and worship.

Prayer

Praise the Lord!
I will give thanks to the Lord with my whole heart,
    in the company of the upright, in the congregation.
Great are the works of the Lord,
    studied by all who delight in them.
Full of honour and majesty is his work,
    and his righteousness endures for ever.
He has gained renown by his wonderful deeds;
    the Lord is gracious and merciful.
He provides food for those who fear him;
    he is ever mindful of his covenant.
He has shown his people the power of his works,
    in giving them the heritage of the nations.
The works of his hands are faithful and just;
    all his precepts are trustworthy.
They are established for ever and ever,
    to be performed with faithfulness and uprightness.
He sent redemption to his people;
    he has commanded his covenant for ever.
Holy and awesome is his name.
The fear of the Lord is the beginning of wisdom;
    all those who practise it have a good understanding.
His praise endures for ever.

Psalm 111

CHAPTER 13

Praying silently

The Spirit helps us in our weakness; for we do not know how to pray as we ought, but that very Spirit intercedes with sighs too deep for words.
Romans 8:26

Jim was a troubled young man who tried to dull his pain with drink and cocaine. These twin addictions meant money was tight and made him a volatile character. One day, raised voices and slammed doors signalled yet another row with his wife, Linda. Their shouting match was about how much they could afford to spend on their daughter Jessica's fifth birthday present. What Jim wanted to buy they could not afford, as Linda had told him forcefully. So, Jim grabbed his coat and drove to the local pub where he drank several pints and a couple of shorts. He could not face going home to be accused, yet again, of wasting money and living recklessly. True though it might be, he was already feeling defeated, and did not need Linda to echo the voice inside his head telling him that he was a loser, and no good. Despite being in no fit state to drive, he headed to his mum's; after all, she would make him a cup of tea and let him sleep the night in the spare room. His phone was on the passenger seat when a text message arrived with a "ping", and he could not resist a quick glance. That was when he lost control of the car and crashed into a tree.

The local vicar heard about this tragic accident a few hours afterwards, when Jim's aunt rang from the hospital to tell him that Jim had just died. He went straight to the hospital. As they stood together by Jim's lifeless body, screened off from the rest of the Accident and Emergency department, Jim's family and friends wanted the vicar to pray. He introduced a time of silence: "Let's remember that God is here, and offer to God our pain and our grief, our disbelief and our questions, our tears and our love for each other." In the background, beyond the curtains, were the sounds of a busy ward, but their shared stillness, heavy with grief, somehow seemed healing. There was a solidarity in those brief moments when everyone's distress, and care for each other, could be experienced and weighed together. This time of relative quiet offered an opportunity for those trying to come to terms with the shocking reality of Jim's death to face their numb disbelief and, in some way, turn to God. The vicar drew this unspoken, poignant togetherness to a close by praying, commending Jim to God, and asking for God's comfort and peace for his family and friends, especially for Linda and Jessica, in the agony of their grief. This prayer gathered the heartache, and the inarticulate anguish felt in the silence, and offered it to God.

Silent prayers collected and presented to God

In the Eucharist, before the Bible readings and the sermon, there is often a short period of praying in silence that concludes with the prayer set for that particular Sunday, known as the Collect. The intention is for the president's invitation ("Let us pray") to be a summons for each member of the congregation to offer their own prayers in the silence. They are invited to lay bare their longings, fears, needs, desires and hurts before God. Each frustration, joy and aspiration offered to God in the stillness is met by the self-giving life and love of God. In the quiet, Christ stands with us, offering what is on our hearts to the Father, and the Father receives our heartfelt prayers with love. This concerted prayer gives an active quality to the silence, and establishes an undercurrent of prayerfulness that continues through the rest of the worship. As the president draws together these prayers and offers them to God in the Collect, the preparation is now complete. The Ministry of the Word can begin; we are ready to listen to God.

Prayer

Tender and compassionate God, you are our steadfast companion throughout our lives. When we rejoice, you celebrate with us; when we are anxious and afraid, you offer us a relationship where we can find the courage to face the unknown; when we weep with sadness, you are our comforter. Help us, O God, to believe that you receive us as we are, and help us to entrust ourselves, with all our many struggles and hopes, to your faithful and abiding care. Amen.

Unknown author

CHAPTER 14

The Word

The Word became flesh and lived among us, and we have seen his glory, the glory as of a father's only son, full of grace and truth.
John 1:14

Once the initial excitement of my new job in the Ministry of Agriculture, Fisheries and Food had worn off, I became convinced that my future lay elsewhere. Besides the frustrations of commuting into London by train, the inevitable argy-bargy of office politics, being desk-bound and a lack of interest in farming, all detracted from my enjoyment of the work. While I conscientiously got on with my tasks, I knew that I was not going to be working in Whitehall for the long term.

Sensing that my restlessness was God preparing me for something else, I began praying that God would show me what I was to do next. At the time, I was reading a book that recommended praying very specifically. Although not entirely convinced of the need for precision, I pleaded with God one dark and misty evening that January as I walked through Horse Guards Parade, "Lord, find me a new post by September. Amen."

Two weeks later, I met up with Graham, a long-standing friend, in Winchester, and in the cathedral told him about my restlessness in my current position but how I was not sure what God was calling me to do next. He responded, "I've been praying too about what you might do, and I was looking at the magazine of the Church Mission Society (CMS), and they're actively looking for teachers. Here, I've cut out the relevant page." In bold print at the top, I read, "Could you answer God's call to teach in Africa or Asia?" I felt a shot of exhilaration and an instant "yes" rise in my heart. I read the rest of the article and noted I had the requisite teaching qualification. I thanked Graham and added, "That's great, Graham. I'll keep this—if that's OK—and give it some thought." I knew that God had spoken directly to me, and that was confirmed through the application and selection process. That September, I was on a plane to Uganda, having been commissioned in Lichfield Cathedral to teach and serve in the school and church of a remote, rural village for two years. Working there was the most formative and enriching period of my life, during which I began to discern a call to ordination, and I look back thankfully to God's word to me through my friend Graham, when I was looking for guidance.

God speaks to us

In the same way that you would get to know me through what I tell you about myself in conversation, God is revealed to us as God speaks to us through the Bible readings and the sermon—the Ministry of the Word— which comes next in the Eucharist.

Each time we speak and listen to each other, we sustain and renew our relationship with one another. Every conversation is a mutual invitation to know each other better, and to strengthen our relationship. Likewise, each time God speaks to us, God invites us to know Christ better and to share in God's life more fully through him. This implicit invitation is to be made explicit in our preaching.

When I was learning to preach in my first post after ordination, the vicar gave me a useful maxim to follow when it came to two principle preaching themes. He told me, "Tell them on twenty-four Sundays that God loves them as they are. On the twenty-fifth Sunday, tell them that they need to change." He was making a point about where the stress is to be placed in our preaching, but he was very aware too that these two messages are related: only by being reassured of God's love do we gain the courage and resolve to embrace new life in Christ in the power of the Spirit. That phrase "in the power of the Spirit" is important: preachers may urge us to grit our teeth and try harder but they serve us best when they emphasize our need to relinquish our self-reliance and turn to Christ. Only by letting go of our striving and straining to please God can we discover a greater dependence on God which is the route to transformation. Whereas our resolve to follow Christ is commendable, it is only effective if its outworking is a greater readiness to receive God's love in Christ into our hearts by the Holy Spirit (Romans 5:5). Eschewing self-sufficiency, we are to cultivate the receptivity and confidence in the Spirit that is essential to our growth in faith, hope and love.

Knowing Christ through the Bible

Through the Scriptures, we enter the mystery of Christ. Words, pictures and stories present Christ to us, and understanding how biblical texts speak of him is vital to knowing Christ (John 5:39).

Besides Christ being the focal point and the fulfilment of the Scriptures, he is also the One who opens our hearts to understand them (Luke 24:32,45). When we let Christ interpret the Bible for us, we see that it speaks of him and his Passion. Since the Holy Spirit, who is the Spirit of Christ, has breathed the Scriptures, we are to understand every passage in the light of Christ, and his death and resurrection (2 Timothy 3:16).

As we read through the biblical story, we see that Christ is its beginning and end. We also note that the recurrent themes of the Scriptures culminate in Christ. Let us recount the overarching narrative of the Bible, sometimes known as salvation history. Creation is brought into being through Christ (Colossians 1:15–16). Following the Fall, God's plan of salvation begins with the call of Abraham (Genesis 3, 12). God's rescue from bondage and oppression in Egypt—the Exodus—is the formative event for God's people. However, God's people repeatedly fail to live up to their calling to represent God's character to the world by embodying peace and justice—*shalom*—in their national life. In the sixth century BC, the ransacking of Jerusalem, the razing of the temple to the ground, and exile in Babylon are understood to be God's judgement on Israel's unfaithfulness. The dissonance between their identity as God's people and their distress, both as refugees in a foreign land and on their return home as a subjugated people, makes their longing for the Messiah ever stronger. This wait generates the narrative tension in the biblical story. The question is always, "When will the Messiah come?" With each successive crisis, the yearning and expectation of God's people gathers pace.

In Jesus Christ, the vocation of God's people is finally fulfilled. Their calling to be the "Light to the Nations" is realized in Christ, who declares himself and the community that gathers around him to be "the Light of the World".[52] Israel's history, marred by unfaithfulness to God, is reworked through his faithfulness. For example, Israel and Christ are both tested in the wilderness. Whereas Israel disobeyed God, Christ resists temptation and remains steadfast.[53] By his constant devotion to God, Christ redeems Israel's waywardness and fulfils Israel's vocation by exemplifying God's character to the world.

Through Christ's obedience to God, even to death on the cross, humanity is refashioned. Our distorted humanity is remoulded by Christ in the white-hot love of God, and this recasting of our humanity reaches its climax at the cross. Here in the crucible of Calvary, the love of God is at its hottest and the reshaping of our humanity most intense. Christ's "yes" to God in his crucifixion is humanity's eternal "yes" to God.

In the Passion of Christ, the themes and stories of the Old Testament are fulfilled. The suffering of the innocent that was the cause of despair, tension and offence throughout Israel's history is resolved in the resurrection of the suffering, innocent servant of God (Isaiah 53:7; Matthew 27:11–14). Initiated into Christ's death and resurrection through baptism and by faith, our humanity is renewed, and Christ's life and faithfulness become ours. Belonging to the Church, we are co-partners with Christ in God's mission and look forward to the End, the joining of heaven and earth in God's kingdom where Christ is enthroned and worshipped (Revelation 21 and 22).

The Bible, therefore, points us forward to the end when earth and heaven will be united in Christ, and humanity will be gathered together in the worship of God (Ephesians 1:9–10). In the Eucharist, this consummation of God's loving purposes is anticipated. We pray for the fulfilment of God's plan, yet also find ourselves in God's kingdom.

Meeting Christ in the Scriptures

As we reflect on our encounter with Christ through the Bible readings and sermon, and through the bread and wine we share together, the experience of the two disciples who encountered the Risen Christ on the road to Emmaus is instructive. They heard the Risen Christ open the Scriptures to them, which led to the meal that they shared with their new-found companion, and informed their insight into the identity of this stranger as he "broke the bread". When Jesus spoke to them of "Moses and all the prophets" and "interpreted to them the things about himself in all the Scriptures", they said to each other, "Were not our hearts burning within us?" (Luke 24:27,32). They saw that his Passion was "in accordance with the Scriptures" (1 Corinthians 15:3–4). When he "blessed and broke" the bread at the evening meal, they recognized him, and then he vanished from their sight. Their encounter with him was fleeting, yet energizing, and left them longing to meet with him again.

Every time the first disciples met with the Risen Christ, they experienced grace. Despite their cowardice being thrown into stark relief by the courage that Jesus displayed in his Passion, they knew renewal and fresh hope. Their desertion of him in his ordeal was forgiven. In these converting encounters, the broad sweep of the biblical narrative is encapsulated: the disciples know that they are sinners, having acted selfishly instead of lovingly, yet they are forgiven and made new too. When we encounter the Risen Christ through the Bible readings and the preaching, we are also invited to receive God's forgiveness and be renewed. Therefore, a constructive question to ask ourselves each Sunday ahead of hearing the Scriptures and the sermon is: "How are we going to be challenged to change?"

Being with the Risen Christ in the Gospels

In the Eucharist, there is always a Gospel reading. The preaching task at the Eucharist is to elucidate this reading, drawing upon the other Bible readings. In the Gospels, the words and actions of Jesus are interpreted in the light of the resurrection. We know what Jesus did and said through those who were with him, the apostles, who met him, and ate and drank with him after he rose from the dead. Their witness is the foundation of the Church, and, in each generation, the Church returns to the "words and actions" of Jesus Christ, to discern how to live for God in its time and context.

The New Testament writers as a whole seek to express the "event of God"—the incarnation, the death, resurrection and ascension of Christ, and the pouring out of the Holy Spirit at Pentecost—that established the Church. They endeavour too to interpret what it meant to follow Christ for those first Christians in their different locations.

In some churches, we stand for the reading of the Gospel in recognition that the incarnation of God in Christ is the centre of the biblical story. If there is a procession in which the Scriptures are brought from the altar to the centre of the nave, it signifies Christ the Saviour coming forth from the Father into the world to speak to us. The "alleluias" that can greet the Gospel reading announce the coming of Christ to us through the Gospel reading. Since Jesus is the ultimate and supreme Word of God, he is the interpretative key to unlocking the Scriptures; by looking at Jesus in the Gospels, we understand how to read the rest of the Bible.

Maintaining our engagement with the Scriptures beyond the Eucharist

The discipline of reading the Scriptures daily helps us to rise to the challenge of growing into Christlikeness. Attending each day to God's voice through the Scriptures means we become more alert to God speaking to us elsewhere, in the circumstances of life, through the people we meet, and in prayer. As we prioritize our response to God's call to us to grow in love, we learn how to discern amongst the competing demands on our time and energy what God is calling us to do. When we sense that God is asking us to do something specific, there are several questions that we can ask ourselves to help us to decide whether we are are indeed being prompted by God. Are we going to grow in faith as a result? Is it in line with Christ's summons to love God and to love others, even our enemies? Is it going to form us into generous, self-giving people? While recognizing that we are to live sacrificially, do we have the capacity to do it? We might also find it helpful to share our thoughts with a wise and long-standing Christian who can be a conversational partner as we seek God's guidance.

Reading and reflecting on the Bible helps us to combat the influence of the surrounding culture, its priorities and prejudices. Since the goal of our reading is that we may cooperate more fully with God, we read carefully and prayerfully, asking for the guidance of the Holy Spirit. Our desire is to deepen our prayer and strengthen our service of God: we are not merely looking to acquire more religious knowledge. A short, well-digested daily reading is a good staple diet. Our Bible reading can be helpfully supplemented by books on theology, prayer and biographies of Christians.

Preaching and the formation of God's people

Sermons are always contextual: different aspects of the unchanging gospel need to be drawn out to address the local and contemporary setting. The preaching task is to announce that the kingdom of God has come in Christ, to deepen people's confidence in Christ, and to assure them that the Holy Spirit is at work in their lives, and the lives of those for whom they pray.

The sermon must aim to consolidate God's work of forming us into Christlike people and be designed to keep our hearts open to God. Irenaeus wrote: "The work of God is the fashioning of a human being."[54] In Genesis, we read, "the Lord God formed man from the dust of the ground, and breathed into his nostrils the breath of life; and the man became a living being" (Genesis 2:7). On Easter Day, the Risen Christ met with his disciples, breathed on them, and said, "Receive the Holy Spirit." Thus a new humanity in Christ was created (John 20:22). In baptism by faith and in the power of the Holy Spirit, we are initiated into this new humanity, and a work of transformation begins. The fashioning of us into the likeness of Christ continues as we take up our cross daily and remain responsive to God's work in our lives (Luke 9:23). We are to learn to acquire the mind and the will of the Risen Christ. This means that the old, this-worldly, individualistic self must die. We must rise into a communion of life with God and our brothers and sisters in Christ. The basic rule of life for the Christian disciple is: "Whatever you do, in word or deed, do everything in the name of the Lord Jesus, giving thanks to God the Father through him" (Colossians 3:17).

A church is a school in discipleship, and the sermon is integral to the formation of humble, self-forgetful disciples. The preacher and the listener collaborate in this task, recognizing their different roles but also their mutual responsibility for each other's growing maturity as followers of Christ. Each time we listen to the Bible readings followed by the sermon, we seek to cultivate an abiding dependence on God by listening attentively, being receptive and ready to respond. Before and during the sermon, we are to pray for the preacher. The goal of the preacher is that the hearers' faith will be strengthened, and that they become more Christlike. Both the preacher and those listening are to aspire to be surrendered and to set their hearts solely on God. Evelyn Underhill, a great twentieth-century writer on prayer, in her book *The Mystery of Sacrifice*, describes an unencumbered heart as "cleansed of delusions, images, and attachments, truly poor, truly chaste, truly obedient, and therefore ready for the invasion of love".[55] This naked faith, stripped of self-interest, is seen in Jesus at the point of death as he cries with a loud voice, "Father, into your hands I commend my spirit" (Luke 23:46). Habakkuk, the prophet, speaks of loving God despite desperate poverty: "Though the fig tree does not blossom, and no fruit is on the vines; though the produce of the olive fails and the fields yield no food; though the flock is cut off from the fold and there is no herd in the stalls, yet will I rejoice in the Lord; I will exult in the God of my salvation" (Habakkuk 3:17–18). We seek to love God, as God loves us, unconditionally.

Repent and believe the good news

The conclusion of the sermon is to be informed by the climatic instruction at the end of the great summaries of the Christian Gospel made to the assembled crowds in the Acts of the Apostles: "You must repent."[56] On each of these occasions, the preacher rounded off his persuasive argument made for Christ, centred on the cross, the resurrection and the judgement of God, with the rallying cry to repentance. Like those first preachers of the gospel, those who preach today are to call their listeners to turn to God.

"We proclaim Christ crucified" is how Paul summarized his preaching (1 Corinthians 1:23). At the cross, our broken, fragmented lives are healed and unified, and offered to God: we are forgiven and restored. In the resurrection, the Risen Christ is given all authority in heaven and earth (Matthew 28:16–20). We are summoned to place our lives into that of the Risen Christ, and share in God's eternal life, in response to what Christ has done on the cross for us, and to his risen presence.

If we are to conform our lives to the life of the Risen Christ, we need to know his critique of our lives and our society's values. Thus, the preacher over time should seek to bring to light all in our contemporary context that is under God's judgement. This prophetic edge cuts through our complacency and highlights our culture's blind spots. We need to see the world in the light of God's justice and his longing for peace.

The Bible readings and sermon proclaim in our midst Christ crucified and glorified, reigning over the Church. Through the Ministry of the Word, God speaks to our hearts and minds, and makes us responsive to the Eternal Word, who became flesh in Jesus (John 1:14). As our lives resonate with Christ's, the watching and waiting world experiences God's grace and truth, in and through us, to the glory of God.

Prayers

A prayer for the preacher to say before the sermon:

> Father, may these spoken words be faithful to your written word
> and lead us to the living Word, Jesus Christ our Lord. Amen.

A prayer reflecting the importance of the Scriptures in Christian discipleship:

> Blessed Lord,
> who caused all holy Scriptures to be written for our learning:
> help us so to hear them,
> to read, mark, learn and inwardly digest them
> that, through patience, and the comfort of your holy word,
> we may embrace and for ever hold fast
>   the hope of everlasting life,
> which you have given us in our Saviour Jesus Christ,
> who is alive and reigns with you,
> in the unity of the Holy Spirit,
> one God, now and for ever. Amen.[57]

CHAPTER 15

Believing

If you confess with your lips that Jesus is Lord and believe in your heart that God raised him from the dead, you will be saved.
Romans 10:9

I enjoy preaching at weddings. The couple's love is an obvious springboard into talking about God's love. As well as preaching about God's love being the spring and source of the love the couple share, I offer one or two pieces of wisdom, drawn from what I have read about love and marriage. I often cite this maxim: *It is not enough to love, but you must say that you love,* and give the couple this challenge: "Try to say, 'I love you' to each other every day of your marriage."

Similarly, when it comes to our faith in God, it is not enough to believe; we must say that we believe.

We affirm our faith in God, Father, Son and Holy Spirit

In the Eucharist, in response to what God has said to us through the Bible readings and the sermon, we declare together our faith in God by reciting together a creed. The Nicene Creed is the one customarily used at the Eucharist in the Church of England:

We believe in one God,
the Father, the Almighty,
maker of heaven and earth,
of all that is,
seen and unseen.

We believe in one Lord, Jesus Christ,
the only Son of God,
eternally begotten of the Father,
God from God, Light from Light,
true God from true God,
begotten, not made,
of one Being with the Father;
through him all things were made.
For us and for our salvation he came down from heaven,
was incarnate from the Holy Spirit and the Virgin Mary
and was made man.
For our sake he was crucified under Pontius Pilate;
he suffered death and was buried.
On the third day he rose again
in accordance with the Scriptures;
he ascended into heaven
and is seated at the right hand of the Father.
He will come again in glory to judge the living and the dead,
and his kingdom will have no end.

We believe in the Holy Spirit,
the Lord, the giver of life,
who proceeds from the Father and the Son,
who with the Father and the Son is worshipped and glorified,
who has spoken through the prophets.
We believe in one holy catholic and apostolic Church.
We acknowledge one baptism for the forgiveness of sins.
We look for the resurrection of the dead,
and the life of the world to come.
Amen.[58]

In making this public statement of what the Church believes, our faith is strengthened. As we proclaim these tenets of the Christian faith, we recommit ourselves to living by these truths. Pseudo-Dionysius the Areopagite—a theologian and philosopher of the late fifth and early sixth centuries—described the creed as "the universal song of praise".[59] In declaring who God is and what God has done, we remind ourselves of the splendour of our faith.

By this declaration of the Church's faith, we express our belonging to the universal Church. Each gathering for the Eucharist expresses the life and unity of the local church but also looks beyond itself to the universal Church it represents.

As we say the Creed, we proclaim our faith, which is both historical—founded on events in history—and eschatological—directed towards the future and the final accomplishment of God's intention for his creation. The Creed encapsulates the biblical narrative from creation to the coming of God's kingdom. This is our story and provides the overarching context in which our own lives are set. While the Creed can sound esoteric and some of its language may seem inaccessible—it was, after all, compiled in the fourth century in the matrix of the contemporary doctrinal disputes—it informs our self-understanding. It holds and preserves those core truths about humanity, who we are and the meaning of our lives, our identity and purpose: we are created, renewed and loved; we share God's eternal life and belong to God's worldwide Church; we look forward to the coming of the kingdom and the consummation of God's love. These fundamental truths to which the Creed bears witness are the markers by which we navigate our individual lives and our life together. Through the Creed, we make sense of every day of our lives and of our journey from birth to death.

God's story summarised in the Creed is one of many stories that seek to explain humanity's existence and goal. It is the Church's confident claim that the Christian narrative delineated in the Creed is the light by which we judge all others. The Church, therefore, has a responsibility to declare to the world the universal truths expressed in the Creed. Central to this proclamation is Jesus Christ, who he is and what he has done for humanity, and his kingdom. Our public witness to our faith when we recite the Creed in church is to be seen as a preparation for being known to be a Christian in every other place we go. Jesus Christ insisted on the need to declare publicly our commitment to him, especially when challenged. Jesus underlined what is at stake in those testing moments with a stern warning: "Those who are ashamed of me and of my words in this adulterous and sinful generation, of them the Son of Man will also be ashamed when he comes in the glory of his Father with the holy angels" (Mark 8:38). When we are put on the spot about our loyalty to Christ, we must be clear and straightforward that our fundamental commitment is to him. Whereas our faith is intensely personal, it is never private; it is always public, because it is for everyone. Convinced of the uniqueness and universality of Christ, the Church's task is to help all people to call upon Christ. As Paul reminds us in his letter to the church in Rome:

> For one believes with the heart and so is justified, and one confesses with the mouth and so is saved. The scripture says, "No one who believes in him will be put to shame." For there is no distinction between Jew and Greek; the same Lord is Lord of all and is generous to all who call on him. For, "Everyone who calls on the name of the Lord shall be saved."
>
> *Romans 10:10–13*

Prayer

> Give me, O Lord, a steadfast heart, which no unworthy thought can drag downwards; an unconquered heart, which no tribulation can wear out; an upright heart, which no unworthy purpose may tempt aside. Bestow upon me also, O Lord my God, understanding to know thee, diligence to seek thee, wisdom to find thee, and a faithfulness that may finally embrace thee; through Jesus Christ, our Lord.
>
> *Thomas Aquinas*[60]

CHAPTER 16

Interceding

The Spirit helps us in our weakness; for we do not know how to pray as we ought, but that very Spirit intercedes with sighs too deep for words.
Romans 8:26

When I worked as a CMS mission partner in Uganda, I, along with a colleague, another David, taught in the secondary school, co-led the school's Scripture Union club with one of the teachers, and preached in the parish's many churches. The vicar, Elijah, was loved, respected and almost revered by the locals, and as well as being our mentor, he soon became a friend. His wife had borne him thirteen children, the twelfth of which had been called Benjamin in the belief that like the biblical patriarch, the twelfth would be his last. Yet, it was not long before Shem followed.

We got to know all his children but particularly Douglas, who was eight years old when we arrived. We would often see him as he collected water from the local spring or on his way to his school. He was likeable, friendly, and interested in us. He would greet us with a bright smile and ask us the customary question, "How are you?" He would laugh with delight when we took him for a ride on our motorbike.

In our second year there, Douglas caught typhoid. When we visited him in the local hospital where his family were with him, caring for him round the clock, his life seemed to be slipping away. The hospital did not have the ciprofloxacin, the antibiotic he needed. We jumped on our motorbike and sped to the pharmacy in the nearest town and bought some. Despite taking the drug, his recovery remained in doubt. One evening, as he lay listless on his hospital bed, we were praying for him back at our home. We feared that he would not recover, and we ached for his vitality to return. His family were desperate and dreading his death. One of my colleague's prayers made a lasting impression on me and whenever I recall it, I can hear his voice quavering as he expressed our heartfelt plea, "Father, don't let Douglas die." By his plaintive and simple intercessory prayer, we stood in the gap between Douglas' precarious health and our hope for him.

Intercession is a response to God's vision for the Church and the world

Our intercessions are a response, as is the recitation of the Creed, to what God has said to us through the Bible readings and the sermon, the Ministry of the Word. What we have heard from God leads us deeper into God's love for God's Church and God's world. We pray through Jesus Christ, the mediator between God and humanity who lives to make intercession for us (Hebrews 7:25; 9:15).

In a beautiful passage on God's love in his letter to the church in Rome, Paul underlines the truth that Jesus Christ is continually interceding for us. Eloquently expressing his conviction that nothing can separate us from God's love, he insists that Christ is on our side and prays for us: "It is Christ Jesus, who died, yes, who was raised, who is at the right hand of God, who indeed intercedes for us" (Romans 8:34). To belong to Christ is to share his life and that entails interceding with him for God's Church and God's world.

To belong to the Church is to be longing for the coming of God's kingdom; this heartfelt yearning is at the centre of the Lord's Prayer: "Thy kingdom come," we pray. Intercession is sharing in the prayer of Jesus Christ before God with the Church and the world on our hearts. As we intercede, Christ gathers all our concerns and longings into his prayer to the Father. We offer our prayers in faith to God. The efficacy of our prayers does not, though, depend on the strength of our faith but on God's character. As the great missionary to China in the nineteenth century, Hudson Taylor, rightly observed, "The issue is not a greater faith, but faith in a great God."[61] Our intercessory prayers are based on our faith in God and offered in hope. Our hope in God is grounded in the historical evidence for the resurrection and the lived experience of Christians down the centuries. The raising of Christ from death to risen life defines God's activity in the world: what is cast down is lifted up and what is old is renewed.

God's goal for creation is to bring all things to perfection in Christ that God "may be all in all" (1 Corinthians 15:28). By the power of the Holy Spirit, God is at work in events and in long-term developments to bring peace and justice. As Dr Martin Luther King Jr, the great civil rights leader, declared, "The arc of the moral universe is long, but it bends toward justice."[62] In line with this conviction, we pray in the Lord's Prayer, "deliver us from evil".

When we intercede, we are not asking God to intervene because God is not absent, outside looking into our world. On the contrary, God is holding the created order in being. Faithfully, God sustains and cares for creation. That is why we can pray hopefully: we are confident that all circumstances are open to the love of Christ in the Holy Spirit.

God's victory over evil has been secured in Christ. We work and pray in the sure hope that God's plan is to be fulfilled in the coming of the kingdom of God when the loud voice from the throne of God in heaven will proclaim:

> See, the home of God is among mortals. He will dwell with them; they will be his peoples, and God himself will be with them; he will wipe every tear from their eyes. Death will be no more; mourning and crying and pain will be no more, for the first things have passed away.
>
> *Revelation 21:3–4*

Looking for the coming of the kingdom

In the Eucharist, we know the joy of the kingdom and the sovereignty of Christ who has been given "all authority in heaven and on earth" (Matthew 28:18). Confident that the world belongs to Christ, we are taken beyond our own particular concerns to see the world from God's perspective. The jarring dissonance between how the world is and how it is to be compels us to pray. The Holy Spirit helps us to pray, yearning within us for the renewal of the Church and the world (Romans 8:22–3).

As we cooperate with God's work in the Church and world, we are drawn into Christ's life and prayer. Activity and prayer go hand in hand in our collaboration with each other and God in God's mission. We work for what we pray. For instance, we might volunteer at the local food bank and give to Christian Aid, as we ask God to "feed the hungry".

Our offering of intercession is integral to the offering of our lives to Christ. In receiving us, God takes our prayer into God's loving purposes. As we pray, we participate in Christ's self-offering, giving up our own agendas and embracing Christ's. Our prayers become, thereby, instrumental in God's shaping of the future. We pray that God may make us channels of his love, through our prayers and in our actions.

When praying, we endeavour to empathize with those for whom we pray. As we stand in solidarity with those who are sick and those who are starving, we seek to be one with those in distress. Our prayer then becomes a place of encounter with those who suffer and with Christ's identification with them, a sharing in Christ's anguish. In this place of pain, we pray with Christ, who has restored everything, that his restoration may apply here and now.

Evelyn Underhill wrote in her book on the Eucharist, *The Mystery of Sacrifice*, "The soul totally possessed by God is a soul totally possessed by charity."[63] When we intercede, we present the world of sin, sadness and suffering lovingly to God. St Catherine of Siena, a mystic and author of the fourteenth century, captures this integral connection between our love for God and our passionate prayer for others: "The altar is the Table of Holy Desire for the honour of God and for the health and salvation of souls."[64] Intercession expresses and completes our self-giving to God's mysterious purpose. In holding together God's love and our world of injustice, suffering, sin and pain, we enter the agony of the cross and the heartache of God.

As we discover the depth and breadth of God's compassion in prayer, our hearts are enlarged. Rather than shrink back, we are to allow ourselves to be drawn into the Passion of God. As we offer ourselves in intercession, our minds are renewed and our hearts softened, and our priorities begin to coincide with God's (Ezekiel 36:26; Romans 12:2).

Even when our prayers are aligned with God's intentions, our hopes can still be dashed. When my mother was diagnosed with stomach cancer, my initial prayer for her was for healing. Over time and through my prayers, I knew that the focus of my intention needed to change and I started to pray for a good ending, a holy death, for her. My mother was in her sixties when she died, and I recognize that we can feel an even greater dissonance when we are praying for a child who is sick to recover to find those pleas "unanswered".

In a world of war, famine and crimes against humanity, the realization of our prayers for peace and justice seems a long way off, and with each setback seems even more distant. Despite the discomfort, we are to persevere in prayer as Jesus urges us in the parables of the persistent friend and the persevering widow (Luke 11:5–8; 18:1–8).

Our prayers have integrity when we are prepared to do what we can to fulfil them. Our cooperation with God in prayer must be mirrored in our actions. Refusing to baulk at this deep engagement with the pain of others, we embrace the God whose compassion has enfolded our lives and has been known by God's people throughout history. In compassion, God responds to his oppressed people in Egypt and to the great crowd who have been following Jesus:

> "I have observed the misery of my people who are in Egypt; I have heard their cry on account of their taskmasters. Indeed, I know their sufferings, and I have come down to deliver them from the Egyptians, and to bring them up out of that land to a good and broad land, a land flowing with milk and honey . . . "
>
> *Exodus 3:7–8*

> [Jesus said,] "I have compassion for the crowd, because they have been with me now for three days and have nothing to eat."
>
> *Mark 8:2*

The liturgy of the Eucharist reminds us of the central place of intercession in the Church's response to God. The prayers of intercession seek to encompass what is on the hearts of those who have gathered for worship but also to stretch the range of their concern. Even our enemies are to be included in our prayers (Matthew 5:44).

In terms of the approaches to leading intercession in worship, the individual leading the intercessions has the alternatives of addressing God directly, "Father we pray for . . . " or using a series of biddings inviting the people to pray, each one introduced by a phrase such as "Let us pray for . . .". Whether the prayer is offered in the silence between these biddings or directly through the words spoken by the person leading the intercession, we pray that the universal and eternal reign of God may be known in the Church and the world.

Prayer

> We bring before thee, O Lord,
> the troubles and perils of peoples and nations,
> the sighing of the prisoners and captives,
> the sorrows of the bereaved,
> the necessities of strangers,
> the helplessness of the weak,
> the despondency of the weary,
> the failing powers of the aged.
> O Lord, draw near to each, for the sake of Jesus Christ, our Lord.
> *Anselm of Canterbury*[65]

CHAPTER 17

The Body of Christ

We are the body of Christ. In the one Spirit we were all baptized into one body. Let us then pursue all that makes for peace and builds up our common life.[66]

Cycling with three friends from Mizen Head to Malin Head in Ireland, the southernmost to the northernmost point, was an enjoyable adventure. In addition to the four cyclists, there were three others in two cars in support. Their main task was carrying our stuff—clothes and our bike gear—from one overnight stop to another. Besides offering us that practical help, they waved us off each morning, and were there to welcome us when we arrived at our destination. As we rode up the steep ascent to Malin Head and crossed the finishing line, they greeted our arrival with cheers, balloons, chocolate cake and ice-cold champagne.

We cycled about seventy miles or thereabouts each day. There was not much chance to chat as we rode along in a straight line to benefit from streamlining and for safety on the busier roads but we would make the occasional comment—"Wow, look at that view" or 'Shall we take a break soon?" or "We should've taken that turning back there!"— and otherwise enjoyed a companionable silence. To restore our energy levels and take a break from the saddle, we would stop every couple of hours to munch flapjacks and stretch our legs, and took a longer rest over lunch. When one of us had a puncture or was flagging, the other three would offer support, helping with the changing of an inner tube or giving some encouragement. Every evening we would eat out at a local pub and talk about our respective days, the cyclists about the breathtaking scenery, the support team about the sites they had visited. There was a great camaraderie amongst us. Through this venture, our mutual trust and friendship deepened, and when it was time to go our separate ways, there was a shared sadness that our time together had come to an end.

Like this tight-knit community travelling from one end of Ireland to the other, the Church, the Body of Christ, is a people on the move. As each participant on our Irish journey made a contribution to its success, each Christian enriches the Church's life. The goal of our travelling was our arrival at Malin Head; the Church's is the kingdom of God. We celebrated together by the finishing line on that bright sunny afternoon; we will rejoice in God's presence when heaven and earth are joined under God's reign of justice and peace.

The Church is holy, yet sinful

In the Eucharist, after the prayers of intercession, our focus shifts to our life together. Our common life embodies our reconciliation with God and each other in Christ. As we exchange a sign of peace, we express our unity under God, accomplished by Christ on the cross. However, we know that sometimes within a local church, and certainly in the national and worldwide Church, there is division and disunity. Until the kingdom of God comes fully, the Church lives with, but must never be resigned to, this disharmony.

In a world plagued by sin, steeped in injustice, and longing for peace, it is also self-evident that the kingdom of God is not yet here in all its fullness. For the time being, the Church lives in this tension between the "now" and "not yet" of the kingdom of God. By the power of the Holy Spirit, the kingdom of God is present; but Christ, the king, is unacknowledged by many and God's reign is not always evident in the world. This duality is reflected in the Church, which is holy, yet sinful.

When the Church lives up to its calling as the Body of Christ, its actions serve God's justice and peace. Also, when the Church declares its identity as Christ's Body, such as when it baptizes, celebrates the Eucharist, and attends to the Scriptures, the Church's and Christ's actions are fully aligned. However, since the Church does not embody Christ as fully as Christ is embodied in Jesus, the Church's actions do not always reflect Christ's actions. When this is the case, the Church is to repent and pray for renewal. The Church's failings cannot, however, jeopardize the enduring truth that the Church embodies and mediates Christ to the world.

The Church is one in Christ

In the Eucharist, Christ sanctifies his Church, purifying it from sin and rededicating it to God. Through our communion with Christ, we are renewed in love for God, each other and the world. We are re-centred on Christ, refashioned as Christ's Body, and re-energized for service in Christ's world.

The Church is catholic, reflecting the full range of human diversity. Bound together in love, we are rescued from individualism, the scourge of the West that results in so much isolation and loneliness. In God's family, we know we are children of God, with brothers and sisters locally and across the world. As God's children, and the Body of Christ, we offer God's invitation to everyone, everywhere, to know God the Father, to be a child of God, and belong to God's Church (Romans 8:16). God makes this universal offer through us, and seeks to unify humanity in Christ. These verses from the letter to the church in Ephesus express this truth:

> There is one body and one Spirit, just as you were called to the one hope of your calling, one Lord, one faith, one baptism, one God and Father of all, who is above all and through all and in all.
> *Ephesians 4:4–6*

In the world's pain and sin, Christ lives his life of utter self-giving, identifying with those experiencing rejection, loss and pain. Identified with Christ, the Church is to serve those who suffer and those on the margins of society. Besides raising up those ground down by poverty, absolute or relative, the Church must speak out prophetically, challenging the status quo. The Church is to work for the transformation of the systems and structures that oppress and degrade people.

When faced with a gross injustice the Church must speak out, confronting those in power. Called to side with the victims, the Church cannot advocate that oppressor and oppressed be reconciled, until oppression stops. Only when justice is established can there be a settled peace. Therefore the Church's first task is to agitate for justice, rather than urge for an end to protest and contention; to call for peace when there is injustice is to collude with injustice. For example, in South Africa, only once the structural injustice of apartheid had been removed could the work of reconciliation begin.

The Church is an agent of God's reconciling love, working to bring together those separated by conflict. We are committed to healing divisions between groups and individuals, and to seeking the unity of all people. By building bridges and tearing down walls, we help people to cross boundaries, cultural, ethnic and linguistic. As we reflect on the biblical account of the pouring out of the Spirit on Jesus' first followers, we know that we too are aided in this work by the Holy Spirit. The Spirit propelled them onto the streets of Jerusalem to tell the city that Jesus is risen, and representatives of the known world were united in hearing of God's love in Christ (Acts 2:1–11). This scene reflects the Christian vision of the whole of humanity united in Christ that informs and inspires us in God's mission. We start, of course, in our own locality, but we do not lose sight of the universal scope of this ministry of reconciliation (2 Corinthians 5:17–20).

The Body of Christ and the life of Christ

In John's Gospel, we see the intimate relationship between Christ and his Church: "I am the vine, you are the branches" (John 15:5). As the vine's life runs through the branches, Christ's life courses through the Church.

Grafted into Christ, we find that we are a new creation, the pioneering members of a renewed humanity (2 Corinthians 5:17). By the Holy Spirit, we are conformed to the image of Christ and renewed daily (Romans 8:29). We serve as Christ serves us; we welcome others as Christ has welcomed us; we live for him and not for ourselves; we forgive as Christ forgives us; and we love as Christ loves us.[67] We share too in Christ's priesthood, praying with him for the Church and the world.

Incorporated in baptism and by faith into the Body of Christ, we are under the direction of the Son, and are related through the Son to the Father. When I was being prepared for baptism and confirmation, I remember the comparison being made between an individual belonging to Christ and a hotel under new ownership. As the staff would expect the hotel's values, décor and ethos to be changed by the incoming manager, those who commit themselves to Christ should be ready for their lives to be transfigured. Aspects of Jesus' activity become our activity instantly—most dramatically the prayer Jesus offers, "Abba, Father", becomes ours—and others become ours over time, such as a readiness to be with those who struggle in our communities (Romans 8:15; Galatians 4:6).

The Body of Christ and the world

As Paul tells us, the Church is to proclaim the gospel of Christ to the world: "We are ambassadors for Christ, since God is making his appeal through us; we entreat you on behalf of Christ, be reconciled to God" (2 Corinthians 5:20). As the Body of Christ, we work and pray for everyone everywhere to flourish and find fulfilment in Christ. We are motivated by our conviction that Christ is unique and his offer of eternal life universal, and by our desire that others come to share our experience of belonging to a loving community, one characterized by mutuality and interdependence, the Body of Christ.

The Church's central place in the created order arises out of Christ's exaltation. Having been given "all authority on earth and heaven" and "the name above every name", Christ exercises his rule in and through the Church, seeking to "gather up all things in him, things in heaven and things on earth".[68] This is an outworking of the resurrection and the gift of the Spirit: Christ's embodied life expands beyond incarnation to include the life of the believing community, and, ultimately, the cosmos itself (see 1 Corinthians 15 and Romans 8). Christ's action of drawing the created order into unity is central to the Eucharist. In this act of worship, the place and people are permeated and pervaded by the Holy Spirit, giving us a foretaste of the end of time when Christ will fill "all things" (Ephesians 4:10).

The Body of Christ and the communion of saints

The communion of saints is the countless company of disciples who have gone before us into heaven. They share with those on earth the same life in the same Spirit. Their example and teaching continue to inspire us, and they cheer us along in our own journey of faith (Hebrews 12:1–2). Amongst them are some that we know by name because their holy lives or heroic faith have brought them to the public's attention, their fame resulting from their openness to the Holy Spirit, and their transparency to Christ. When we celebrate the witness of a particular saint, we reverence Christ's life, which is within them and within us. We look to learn from their lives how to deepen our dependence on the Holy Spirit, and to give ourselves more fully to God.

As we reflect on the Body of Christ in the light of the communion of saints, we may find contemplating Mary, the mother of Jesus, to be singularly instructive. The angel Gabriel tells Mary, "The Holy Spirit will come upon you, and the power of the Most High will overshadow you; therefore the child to be born will be holy; he will be called Son of God." She responds, "Here am I, the servant of the Lord; let it be with me according to your word" (Luke 1:35–8). As her humanity was indwelt by God, Christ's presence is within the Church—though not constrained within the Church. As the Holy Spirit fills Mary, the Church is likewise imbued by the Spirit as a sign and anticipation of the entire creation being suffused by the Spirit. Mary accepts her vocation, and is filled with the Holy Spirit. Whereas her unique calling is to be the mother of Jesus Christ, we see humanity's universal calling realized in her: each human being is created in the image of God to be the temple of the Holy Spirit, the place where the Spirit of God dwells.

Mary is also an exemplar of Christian discipleship for she goes on her own pilgrimage of faith, following Jesus all the way to the cross. Mary trusted God and God's word, and, therefore, found the meaning and the fulfilment of her life, in God. By her adoration of Jesus and her love for him, Mary represents each disciple's devotion; in her delight at knowing him, she personifies the joy of the Church. Every evening, the Church sings her great song of praise and elation, the Magnificat: "My soul magnifies the Lord, and my spirit rejoices in God my Saviour" (Luke 1:46–7).

The peace

The exchange of a sign of peace in the Eucharist—usually a handshake—signifies that in Christ humanity and God are reconciled. It is a symbolic act through which we express this unity and those with whom we exchange a sign of peace represent the whole of humanity. In these brief but meaningful interactions, we express the truth that we have been released from the guilt of past failings, restored and bound together in one community, the Body of Christ.

Vincent Donovan discovered through his relationship with the Masai tribe in Kenya a ritual of reconciliation which has obvious parallels with the Eucharist:

> Sometimes the sin occurs, not between individuals, but among groups in the same community. One family might offend another family, and disruption sets in on the whole community. If possible, both the offending and offended family must be brought back together by an act of forgiveness sought and bestowed. So, at the behest of the total community, both families prepare food. The word for food in Masai is *endaa*. But this will be a special kind of food called *endaa sinyati*, meaning *holy food*. This holy food is brought to the centre of the village by the two families, accompanied by the rest of the community encouraging both families along the way. There in the centre of the village, the food is exchanged between the two families, each family accepting the food prepared by the other family. Then the holy food is eaten by both families, and when it is, forgiveness comes, and the people say that a new *osotua* has begun. *Osotua* is the word for covenant or pact of testament. A New Testament of forgiveness is brought about by the exchange of food.[69]

Our love for each other confirms the presence of Christ in our midst, so the quality of each church's common life matters profoundly. Summoned to love with divine love, we are to be known as Christ's disciples by this love that we share (John 13:35). The love of Christ is the origin and distinctive sign of the Church. That is why division and enmity within and between churches mar the credibility of our faith, and the converting power of the Church's witness to Christ.

The liturgical action of sharing the peace also signals our commitment to live in peace and to make peace. Fundamentally disposed to affirm each other, we approach those beyond the Church with the same generous attitude. Our love for our brothers and sisters in Christ is expressed in mutual service through which everyone discovers their gifts and their ministry in the life of the Church.

Our aim, when we are together and when we are dispersed, is for our faith and our actions to match up. Living an integrated life where our love for Christ is seen consistently in every facet of our lives is our goal. Individually and together, we want to be known as trustworthy people. When a church's life and witness resonate, then those who encounter the church are impressed and predisposed to consider the gospel.

In Christ, we share in Christ's reconciling work, and witness to Christ's love by fulfilling the new commandment: "Just as I have loved you, you should also love one another" (John 13:34). Seeking to love by restoring strained relationships, we will be led to play our part in resolving conflicts within and beyond the Church. Jesus said, "Blessed are the peacemakers, for they will be called children of God" (Matthew 5:9). In our own lives, we will, while maintaining our integrity, strive to be on good terms with everyone. In Romans, Paul urges, "If it is possible, so far as it depends on you, live peaceably with all" (Romans 12:18).

Prayer

> Christ has no body on earth but yours,
> No hands but yours,
> No feet but yours;
> Yours are the eyes through which Christ
> must look with compassion on the world.
> Yours are the feet with which he is to go about doing good,
> and yours are the hands with which he is to bless now.
>
> *Attributed to Teresa of Avila*[70]

CHAPTER 18

The Eucharistic Prayer

When he was at the table with them, he took bread, blessed and broke it, and gave it to them. Then their eyes were opened, and they recognized him; and he vanished from their sight.

Luke 24:30–1

I have been an associate of the Anglican monastery, the Community of the Servants of the Will of God, in Crawley Down in Sussex for over thirty years. When I go there on retreat, although I value the silence and solitude, the highlight is always the worship, especially the daily Eucharist. For the Eucharistic Prayer, we gather at the front of the chapel where the famous icon of the Trinity by Rublev hangs on the wall behind the altar. As the priest invites us to "lift up our hearts", we are in the presence of the triune God. Basking in God's love, we respond to the invitation to "give thanks" with "it is right to give thanks and praise".[71] In this great prayer of gratitude and love for God, we fulfil our eternal purpose and know the meaning of our lives. Standing together, guests and monks, circled around the altar, facing the icon, we are thankful for each other, and the intimacy and holiness of God, who is Father, Son and Holy Spirit.

The Great Prayer of Thanksgiving

As we pray the Eucharistic Prayer, we offer ourselves to God in Christ, sharing in Christ's self-offering. While Christ's entire life is dedicated to God, his obedience becomes more demanding from the start of his public ministry at his baptism onwards and reaches a climax in his death on the cross. Close to his death, Jesus prays, "'Now my soul is troubled. And what should I say—"Father, save me from this hour"? No, it is for this reason that I have come to this hour. Father, glorify your name.' Then a voice came from heaven, 'I have glorified it, and I will glorify it again'" (John 12:27–8). In John's Gospel, Christ's crucifixion is intrinsic to one upward movement that includes his resurrection and ascension, whereby Christ is exalted. In our commemoration of Christ's Passion and return in triumph to the Father in the Eucharist, we are caught up in this movement and ascend into the Father's presence in the kingdom of God. We are drawn into Christ's perpetual self-offering, eternally defined by his death, resurrection and ascension.

In the Eucharistic Prayer, the whole mystery of Christ is unfolded. We give thanks for creation, incarnation, redemption and the gift of the Spirit, and we look forward to the final coming of Christ to unite heaven and earth in the kingdom of God. As we are taken through this summary of the biblical narrative, we offer thanks and praise for God's work in our lives and throughout the entire created order. This work is creative, redemptive—we have been set free—and sanctifying—we are being made holy.

The president acts on behalf of the church—those who have gathered for worship—but it is the entire assembly that prays the prayer. The consecration of the bread and wine, and the offering of the whole of creation with Christ to God, is confirmed by the corporate "Amen" at the end of the prayer.

Although only part of the liturgy of the Church of England since 1980, Eucharistic Prayer B in one of the current books of services and prayers—*Common Worship*—has deep historical roots since it is based on the third-century liturgy of St Hippolytus of Rome, a prominent theologian in the early Church. I shall use this text to consider the classic structure and content of the Eucharistic Prayer.[72] The congregational response is in bold print.

Introductory dialogue

> The Lord be with you
> **and also with you.**

or

> The Lord is here.
> **His Spirit is with us.**

In this great prayer of thanksgiving, we remember God, his gifts to us in creation, and our salvation in Christ. We do, however, need God to inspire our thanks and praise. Therefore, we look to God, the Holy Spirit in our midst, to lead us in prayer.

> Lift up your hearts.
> **We lift them to the Lord.**

By lifting our hearts towards God, we prepare to enter God's kingdom where we rediscover our identity—we are Christ's—and are renewed. "You have died, and your life is hidden with Christ in God" (Colossians 3:3). In the Eucharist, the Church ascends "upwards" and enters the joy of the kingdom of God.

> Let us give thanks to the Lord our God.
> **It is right to give thanks and praise.**

"Thanks and praise" is the right response to God. Thanksgiving transforms our relationship to the world, and by cultivating gratitude as our basic attitude to life, our entire lives become a means of communion with God. As we give thanks, we acknowledge our dependence upon God, making our relationship with God reciprocal: God gives, and we respond with thanks. While we give thanks for specific gifts, our lives are grounded in gratitude to God, who is the source and goal of our lives, and our life together. When we see life and the whole creation as God's gift, our hearts overflow with praise.

The first part of the thanksgiving

> Father, we give you thanks and praise
> through your beloved Son Jesus Christ, your living Word,
> through whom you have created all things;
> who was sent by you in your great goodness to be our Saviour.
>
> By the power of the Holy Spirit he took flesh;
> as your Son, born of the blessed Virgin,
> he lived on earth and went about among us;
> he opened wide his arms for us on the cross;
> he put an end to death by dying for us;
> and revealed the resurrection by rising to new life;
> so he fulfilled your will and won for you a holy people.

Here we offer thanksgiving first for creation, and then redemption, our liberation from death into eternal life. We affirm too that God has given us the kingdom in the resurrection of Christ—the future has been given to us in Christ that it may constitute the life of the Church now. This section of the prayer may conclude with some specific thanks called a "proper preface", reflecting the liturgical season, such as Lent or Easter, or the particular focus of the celebration, for example, on saints' days.

The Sanctus

> Therefore with angels and archangels,
> and with all the company of heaven,
> we proclaim your great and glorious name,
> for ever praising you and saying:
>
> **Holy, holy, holy Lord,**
> **God of power and might,**
> **heaven and earth are full of your glory.**
> **Hosanna in the highest.**

Our thanksgiving flows into the Sanctus, and we participate in the ceaseless worship of heaven, singing with the angels, archangels and the communion of saints. In earth and heaven, the response to God's glory is awe and reverence, and at the End, the whole created order will sing with the Church this eternal song.

The Benedictus

> Blessed is he who comes in the name of the Lord.
> **Hosanna in the highest.**

In his coming into Jerusalem on Palm Sunday, in his coming in the Eucharist, in his coming at the end to reign in his kingdom, the Christ is "the blessed one" who comes in "the name of the Lord".

Calling down the Spirit on the bread and wine

> Lord, you are holy indeed, the source of all holiness;
> grant that by the power of your Holy Spirit,
> and according to your holy will,
> these gifts of bread and wine
> may be to us the body and blood of our Lord Jesus Christ;

This calling down of the Holy Spirit—known as an "epiclesis"—is on the elements, the bread and wine. Suffused and saturated by the Holy Spirit, the bread becomes to us Christ's body and the wine, his blood. This epiclesis is followed by the invocation of the Holy Spirit on God's people at the culmination of the Eucharistic Prayer.

Narrative of institution

> . . . who, in the same night that he was betrayed,
> took bread and gave you thanks;
> he broke it and gave it to his disciples, saying:
> Take, eat; this is my body which is given for you;
> do this in remembrance of me.
> In the same way, after supper
> he took the cup and gave you thanks;
> he gave it to them, saying:
> Drink this, all of you;
> this is my blood of the new covenant,
> which is shed for you and for many for the forgiveness of sins.
> Do this, as often as you drink it,
> in remembrance of me.

We come to one specific night packed with significance and heavy with pathos: the same night that Jesus washed his disciples' feet and told them to "love each other". He urged them to abide in his love, the love that took him to the cross. The sacrifice of his death is the fulfilment of a life through which divine love renews humanity and restores creation. The world is judged by its complicity in Jesus' betrayal and death through which, paradoxically, God saves the world.

As the president offers the bread and wine, imitating Christ at the Last Supper, these gifts to God are taken up into Christ's self-offering to the Father. By his command and promise, the bread and wine are identified with his body and blood. The Lord's word is authoritative, and we respond to Christ's command, "Do this in remembrance of me". As Queen Elizabeth I famously put it:

> "'Twas Christ the Word that spake it,
> the same took bread and brake it,
> and as the Word did make it,
> so I believe and take it."[73]

We commemorate the body-giving and blood-shedding of Christ. His sacrificial death is the climax of a life of self-giving love and defines love for eternity as sacrificial.

Acclamations

One of these four acclamations is used:

>Great is the mystery of faith:
>**Christ has died:**
>**Christ is risen:**
>**Christ will come again.**

or

>Praise to you, Lord Jesus:
>**Dying you destroyed our death,**
>**rising you restored our life:**
>**Lord Jesus, come in glory.**

or

>Christ is the bread of life:
>**When we eat this bread and drink this cup,**
>**we proclaim your death, Lord Jesus,**
>**until you come in glory.**

or

>Jesus Christ is Lord:
>**Lord, by your cross and resurrection**
>**you have set us free.**
>**You are the Saviour of the world.**

These acclamations are the response of the people to the narrative of institution, the recalling of the Last Supper. They also attest to the Eucharist being an evangelistic proclamation of the cross for, as Paul put it, "For as often as you eat this bread and drink the cup, you proclaim the Lord's death until he comes" (1 Corinthians 11:26).

Anamnesis

> And so, Father, calling to mind his death on the cross,
> his perfect sacrifice made once for the sins of the whole world;
> rejoicing in his mighty resurrection and glorious ascension,
> and looking for his coming in glory,
> we celebrate this memorial of our redemption.
>
> As we offer you this our sacrifice of praise and thanksgiving,
> we bring before you this bread and this cup
> and we thank you for counting us worthy
> to stand in your presence and serve you.

This whole section is crafted as a response to Jesus' command to "do this in remembrance of me". It is called "the anamnesis" which is the transliteration from the original Greek, and means "recollection" or "memorial". The latter definition appears in the text above—"we celebrate this 'memorial' of our redemption"—and refers to an act whereby the person or event remembered is made present in the here and now. By recapitulating the life, death and resurrection of Christ, we know Christ in the present, and all the benefits of the Paschal Mystery. In response, we offer the bread and cup as symbols of our lives and the whole of creation, and thank God for his grace in making us his children and servants.

Epiclesis

> Send the Holy Spirit on your people
> and gather into one in your kingdom
> all who share this one bread and one cup,
> so that we, in the company of all the saints,
> may praise and glorify you for ever,
> through Jesus Christ our Lord;

Having made the memorial, the Church looks expectantly to God for the Holy Spirit to be poured out anew. By the Church's obedience to Christ's command—by doing "this" in "remembrance" of Christ—we share in Christ's self-offering and are ready to receive anew the promised Holy Spirit. This epiclesis, commemorating Pentecost, calls down the Holy Spirit on God's people. In the power of the Holy Spirit and in union with Christ, we are offered to the Father and are made new in the kingdom of God.

The Doxology

> ... by whom, and with whom, and in whom,
> in the unity of the Holy Spirit,
> all honour and glory be yours, almighty Father,
> for ever and ever.
> **Amen.**

The prayer ends with praise and adulation. At the climax and culmination of the prayer, the whole of creation and all of time is drawn into Christ's self-offering and presented to God in love (Revelation 22:13). The "Amen" is the Church's assent to what the president has prayed on their behalf. It signals the Church's participation and confirmation of the entire prayer. This concluding doxology is a rising crescendo that reaches its climax in the resounding "Amen".

Prayer

As the night-watch looks for the morning,
so do we look for you, O Christ.
Come with the dawning of the day
and make yourself known in the breaking of the bread. Amen.[74]

CHAPTER 19

Our Father

He set off and went to his father. But while he was still far off, his father saw him and was filled with compassion; he ran and put his arms around him and kissed him.

Luke 15:20

Jesus tells the parable of the waiting father in response to the carping of the Pharisees (Luke 15:11–32). They are outraged by how Jesus eats with "sinners". He tells them this story to explain why he is receiving hospitality from those they ignore, drawing a parallel between his compassion for the "lost" with that of the father for the returning younger son. He also portrays the Pharisees' self-righteousness through the older son in the story, and ends with an implicit invitation to them to think again. By illustrating his ministry through the father's love in the parable, Jesus is implying what we know to be true: Jesus Christ is the Son who reveals the Father.

In giving his younger son his share of the inheritance long before his death, we see the freedom God gives us, and how we are prone to misuse it. When we notice that the father spots the crestfallen son on the distant horizon, we sense that he has been yearning for his return, and looking out for him daily. In the father's heartache, we know God's longing for us to return when we are distant. His extravagant welcome—hug, robe, ring and sandals—speaks to us of God's grace. His lavish party for his prodigal son underlines that God raises his children when they are low, even when it is our foolishness that has led to our downfall. His joy at his son's safe return reveals the passionate commitment of God to each one of us. Therefore, whenever we talk about God the Father, we need to remember this parable and picture the father's generous love for his returning child:

we are to regard "Father" as defined by this parable. When we call God "Our Father", this is the kind of father we are addressing. In the light of the Father's overwhelming love for us, we, confidently, pray, "Our Father in heaven . . . ".

Jesus is the image of the Father: the Father is recognized in the Son

Through the Eucharist, we journey towards the climactic use of Jesus' form of address to God: "Our Father . . . ". After the Eucharistic Prayer, the great prayer of thanksgiving, we are invited to pray together the Lord's Prayer. The boldness to call God "Our Father" is given by the Holy Spirit who has been poured into our hearts, and who draws us ever more deeply into the Son's relationship with the Father. Born from heaven by the Holy Spirit, we are given the prerogative to call God "Abba, Father" (John 3:3; Romans 8:15). This honour of being a child of God is a gift of Christ to us. Like the prodigal son, we return to the Father in each Eucharist and discover each time, with undiminishing joy, that he has come to meet us while we were "still far off" (Luke 15:11–32). As we ascend into the Father's presence, we are welcomed and our arrival is celebrated.

We participate in Christ's relationship with the Father

We are united with Christ in our baptism, and grow into his life and prayer throughout our lives. As Jesus' life and prayer become increasingly ours, we share in his intimacy with the Father, his joy in the Father's presence, and his gratitude to the Father. His God has become our God, his Father has become our Father, and when we cry, "Abba! Father!" it is the Holy Spirit bearing witness within us that we are children of God (John 20:17; Romans 8:16). Through the Holy Spirit, we live in Christ and Christ lives in us. Through this mutual indwelling, we share Christ's life, participating both in the risk and darkness of Christ's death, and the security and light of Christ's resurrection.

As a child of God, we can enjoy the privilege of prayer. Jesus said, "Whenever you pray, go into your room and shut the door and pray to your Father who is in secret; and your Father who sees in secret will reward you" (Matthew 6:6). In this decision to give time to God, we prioritize our relationship with God over all competing demands. Alone before God in prayer, we cooperate with God's work of strengthening our faith, hope and love, the theological virtues, that are grounded in God, and have God as their goal. Spending time with God in solitude is a springboard to repeatedly turning to God, if only momentarily, throughout the day. By praying alone and punctuating our lives with prayer, we learn to trust in the providence of our Father. Praying with others, and for others in their presence, are other modes of prayer that can strengthen our faith and deepen our Church's life. Authentic prayer, however we pray, is the gateway to a deeper love for people and a greater commitment to a life of service. A developing reliance on God in prayer enables us to say "yes" to God whatever God is asking of us. We trust the Father to give us the Holy Spirit when we ask and have a childlike confidence in his goodness (Matthew 7:11; Luke 11:13).

Starting and ending the day in prayer is a good discipline. Offering the day ahead of us, when we wake, and giving thanks for the day that has ended before we sleep, enfolds the day in prospect and retrospect, in prayer. When our sleep is fitful, or we wake up in the night and struggle to get back to sleep, instead of fretting, we can pray. Thereby, the whole of life becomes prayerful. As our lives increasingly conform to God's will and action, then, as Origen—a theologian in the third century—poetically put it, "The whole of our life says, 'Our Father.'"[75]

The use of "our" at the start of the Lord's Prayer indicates its corporate dimension. We, the family of God, pray "Our Father"; it is the joy of the whole worldwide Church. Our privilege to respond to God as a child to a loving parent is allied to an obligation to work and pray for those who do not yet know God as "Father" to come to know God as the Father of our Lord Jesus Christ. Therefore, when we pray "Our Father", we look in hope for the day when everyone, everywhere will be able to pray it in unison.

By daring to utter "Our Father", we promise to be there for God as God is there for us. Our readiness to receive the bread and wine, the body and blood of Christ, depends on our being able to say the Lord's Prayer with longing and integrity. As we pray for the coming of the kingdom, we pledge to work for the common good, living in the hope of the End when "peace and justice" will come, and to work for the well-being and unity of the whole of humanity. St Cyprian, a third-century bishop of Carthage and writer, in his treatise on the Lord's Prayer, explains how the Church prays for and on behalf of the whole of humanity which is united under God's providential care: "Our prayer is public and for all, and when we pray, we pray not for a single person but the whole people, because we are all one."[76]

Prayer

Our Father in heaven,
hallowed be your name,
your kingdom come,
your will be done,
on earth as in heaven.
Give us today our daily bread.
Forgive us our sins
as we forgive those who sin against us.
Lead us not into temptation
but deliver us from evil.
For the kingdom, the power,
and the glory are yours
now and for ever.
Amen.[77]

CHAPTER 20

Being fed

Bread of Heaven,
Bread of Heaven,
feed me till I want no more,
feed me till I want no more.[78]

I was born when my parents were living in a second-floor flat in Herne Hill in London in 1960. In my first year, they expected some sleep deprivation, but they had a long succession of broken nights when my crying was persistent, and they could not get me settled. Exhausted and feeling as though they were failing parents, and not knowing where else to turn, they went to see their GP. After checking that I was not sick, too hot or too cold at night, did not have colic or anything else wrong with me, he decided that my nightly bawling was just down to being hungry. He told them to try doubling the concentration of my feeds, to put in twice the recommended amount of milk powder into the hot water, and if that did not work to come back. His diagnosis was spot on and the remedy worked a treat. I was no longer woken by hunger pangs and started to sleep through the night. After a week or so, my mum and dad were feeling rested, and suitably buoyed up.

Being fed as a baby is fundamental to the human experience. In that early stage of life, we are all utterly dependent on others giving us food for our survival. When we know that all food is a gift from God, we see that what we readily accept is true for babies is true for humanity in general: we need to be fed.

God's people fed by God in the wilderness

Traipsing through the barren landscape of the wilderness, God's people were struggling to find food. They harked back to their time in Egypt when, as they complained to their leaders, their taste buds were excited and their bellies always full. At night, they dreamed of fish, cucumbers, melons, onions and garlic (Numbers 11:5). They questioned whether God was capable of providing for them in this bleak terrain, saying to Moses and Aaron, "'If only we had died by the hand of the Lord in the land of Egypt, when we sat by the fleshpots and ate our fill of bread; for you have brought us out into this wilderness to kill this whole assembly with hunger.' Then the Lord said to Moses, 'I am going to rain bread from heaven for you, and each day the people shall go out and gather enough for that day'" (Exodus 16:3–4).

God did provide "bread from heaven" and their hunger was satisfied. When the nearest sources of water were out of reach, their throats parched and their mouths dry, God again provided. "He made water flow for you from flint rock, and fed you in the wilderness with manna that your ancestors did not know, to humble you and to test you, and in the end to do you good" (Deuteronomy 8:15–16).

God also provided food for a large crowd through the prophet Elisha. Despite having barely enough food to feed twenty people, Elisha insisted that his loaves of bread and the ears of grain be set before the one hundred people present. His faith in God's provision proved justified (2 Kings 4:42–4).

The Eucharist and feeding the hungry

Following the example of Moses and Elisha, Jesus looks to God to help him to feed a large crowd, which in his case was the thousands of people who were following him through the Galilean countryside.[79] He takes the bread he is given, blesses God, breaks the loaves and shares them, the typical actions of the host at a Jewish family meal. We can speculate that when Jesus broke bread at the Last Supper, some of those present might have recalled other occasions when Jesus took bread and prayed to God, and remembered how Jesus fed a multitude with some bread and a few fish. We can extend the link between this feeding miracle and the Last Supper to the Eucharist; they are all interconnected through the presence of Jesus, the prayer he offered at the "breaking of bread," and by those gathered being fed.

In a vivid portrayal of the Judgement of the Nations, Jesus emphasizes that the Church is called to feed the hungry (Matthew 25:42). When we eat bread in the Eucharist, we cannot be unaware that bread is food and that many in our world are hungry. Our eating of bread in the Eucharist prompts in us a concern for those who have no bread. Our hunger for God met in the Eucharist provokes a corresponding hunger for justice.

Jesus meets our hunger for God

Following the feeding miracle in John's Gospel, Jesus eludes the crowds who want to force him to be king. He withdraws, but they are not deterred and continue to search for him. When they find Jesus, he turns their attention from their stomachs to their hearts. They pursue Jesus because he can satisfy their physical hunger, but he tells them that more importantly, he can meet their hunger for God. He draws a contrast between bread that can go stale and the food that he can give that "endures to eternal life" (John 6:27). By believing that Jesus is the one sent by God, they can have food that always gives life, eternal life. This abundant life is a sharing in God's life, an experience of the kingdom of God here and now, and an anticipation of God's reign on earth at the End. This means that we need not fear death because Jesus promises to lead us through death into eternity (John 6:25–35). The food that he gives is the bread and wine, his body and blood, of the Eucharist; it is the food of eternal life. We enter eternal life in baptism and by faith; we are sustained in eternal life, by eating his flesh and drinking his blood:

> Unless you eat the flesh of the Son of Man and drink his blood, you have no life in you. Those who eat my flesh and drink my blood have eternal life, and I will raise them up on the last day; for my flesh is true food and my blood is true drink. Those who

> eat my flesh and drink my blood abide in me, and I in them. Just as the living Father sent me, and I live because of the Father, so whoever eats me will live because of me.
>
> *John 6:53–7*

Here Jesus draws a direct link between taking the bread and wine in the Eucharist into our bodies and his dwelling in us and with us. There is a vital relationship between eating the body and drinking the blood of Christ, and knowing Christ through whom our hunger for God is met:

> Jesus said to them, 'I am the bread of life. Whoever comes to me will never be hungry, and whoever believes in me will never be thirsty.'
>
> *John 6:35*

Knowing Christ in the "breaking of the bread"

Luke and John share the same conviction that the Risen Jesus meets us in the bread of the Eucharist. Their understanding of the Eucharist is implicit in two famous post-resurrection appearances of Jesus. Luke tells of two disheartened disciples trudging along the road from Jerusalem to Emmaus; they are joined by a stranger who walks with them and engages them in conversation about recent events in the city. When they relay their dismay at Jesus' crucifixion and their scepticism at the rumours of his resurrection, he explains to them from the Scriptures that the Messiah had to suffer and to die, before "entering into his glory". Having persuaded the stranger to stay with them, they sit to eat together, and when the stranger "took bread, blessed and broke it, and gave it to them", they knew him. Jesus is revealed in the "breaking of bread" (Luke 24:13–35). The stranger on the way has become their companion, the one with whom they break bread.

In John's telling of the story of the miraculous catch of fish, the disciples are mystified by the individual on the lakeshore, who has told these wily fishermen where to lower their net in the lake to catch the fish that have evaded them all night long. Their recognition of Jesus coincides with his breaking of the bread:

> When they had gone ashore, they saw a charcoal fire there, with fish on it, and bread. Jesus said to them, "Bring some of the fish that you have just caught." So Simon Peter went aboard and hauled the net ashore, full of large fish, a hundred and fifty-three of them; and though there were so many, the net was not torn. Jesus said to them, "Come and have breakfast." Now none of the disciples dared to ask him, "Who are you?" because they knew it was the Lord. Jesus came and took the bread and gave it to them, and did the same with the fish. This was now the third time that Jesus appeared to the disciples after he was raised from the dead.
>
> *John 21:9–14*

The stranger on the shore has become their companion—the one with whom they break bread.

In the Eucharist, we are "exalted"

In addition to Jesus' feeding miracles, the New Testament passages that relate to communal meals have a bearing on how the Church celebrates the Eucharist.

For example, Luke tells us that when we come to eat with Jesus, those who are ostracized by wider society are welcome. No one who responds to Jesus' invitation is to be excluded:

> After this he went out and saw a tax-collector named Levi, sitting at the tax booth; and he said to him, "Follow me." And he got up, left everything, and followed him. Then Levi gave a great banquet for him in his house; and there was a large crowd of tax collectors and others sitting at the table with them. The Pharisees and their scribes were complaining to his disciples, saying, "Why do you eat and drink with tax-collectors and sinners?" Jesus answered, "Those who are well have no need of a physician, but those who are sick; I have come to call not the righteous but sinners to repentance."
>
> *Luke 5:27–32*

We are to interpret Jesus' answer to the Pharisees and scribes as founded on the truth that only those who repent are ready to receive God's grace; just as only those who know they are sick go to see a doctor, only those aware of their sin are going to be ready to turn to God through Jesus. Later in Luke's Gospel, Jesus reminds us that we need to come to the Eucharist humbly, laying aside any pretension or social standing, for then we will be lifted up:

> When you are invited, go and sit down at the lowest place, so that when your host comes, he may say to you, "Friend, move up higher", then you will be honoured in the presence of all who sit at the table with you. For all who exalt themselves will be humbled, and those who humble themselves will be exalted."
>
> *Luke 14:10–11*

After receiving the bread and wine, his body and blood, we thank God for feeding us with the food we need for eternal life. Our relationship with God having been nourished and our resolve to live for God strengthened, we now offer ourselves to God's service. Our hunger for God has been met; our hunger for justice accentuated.

Prayer

> Almighty God,
> we thank you for feeding us
> with the body and blood of your Son Jesus Christ.
> Through him we offer you our souls and bodies
> to be a living sacrifice.
> Send us out
> in the power of your Spirit
> to live and work
> to your praise and glory. Amen.[80]

CHAPTER 21

Going

Go in peace to love and serve the Lord.[81]

At the graduation ceremony for medical students at the University of Leicester, one of their number strides to the podium, and leads the latest cohort of junior doctors in the physicians' pledge of the World Medical Association. It begins:

> As a member of the medical profession:
> I solemnly pledge to dedicate my life to
> the service of humanity;
> The health and wellbeing of my patient
> will be my first consideration;
> I will respect the autonomy and dignity of my patient;
> I will maintain the utmost respect for human life . . .

and concludes,

> I make these promises solemnly, freely, and upon my honour.

Hearing these individuals make this declaration, you feel the weight of the responsibility to their profession and their patients they now bear. These promises are the markers of a life dedicated to others. Their gravity, and the sacrifices they anticipate, is appreciated by those who listen, and at the end of the pledge, these new junior doctors are hailed by a loud and prolonged round of applause. At the culmination of five years of study, the university is confident that they have been formed as doctors and are equipped to go on to hospital wards to begin their work.

Like medical training, the Eucharist forms us ready for service in the world. In the prayer after communion, we offer ourselves to God as "living sacrifices" and are ready to be dispersed to our various settings to live out our discipleship. It can be argued that the purpose of the Eucharist is realized at its end, when we are sent out into God's mission. That's why the Eucharist is called the Mass in the Roman Catholic Church (and in some parts of the Anglican Church too)—which is derived from the ecclesiastical Latin for the dismissal, the "sending out". Before we go, we promise in the name of Christ to love and serve God.

Collaborating with God in God's mission

Before we are sent out into the world, we are assured of God's blessing. The president pronounces the blessing of God, Father, Son and Holy Spirit, in recognition of all that has been given to us by God in the Eucharist, and in anticipation of the dismissal when we are sent out into the world to serve God.

When Jesus commissions his first followers to "make disciples of all nations, baptizing them in the name of the Father, Son, and Holy Spirit," he assures them of the blessing of his presence as they go out into the world to share in God's mission: " . . . remember, I am with you always, to the end of the age" (Matthew 28:16–20). The command to baptize reflects God's invitation to everyone to belong to God's worldwide family. Those who accept this invitation and are baptized share in the life of God. The reference to the "end of the age" points to when creation will be renewed and the whole of humanity united in God's love (Habakkuk 2:14; Colossians 1:19–20). Our looking forward to the End brings a restless quality to Christian discipleship; we can never be entirely satisfied with the status quo. We have to balance a basic contentment with our lives with our yearning for the transformation of ourselves, the Church and the world. When we are in danger of becoming too comfortable, the Holy Spirit disturbs us, urging us to seek the kingdom of God anew. Our prayer that God's will be done on earth as in heaven expresses and reminds us of the future orientated nature of our faith.

We pray and work for what God has achieved in Christ to be realized in a renewed creation and a just and peaceful world. As our prayers and actions are inspired and enfolded in the Spirit, we participate in God's mission, which is local and global. Having known the fire of God's love in the Eucharist, we are sent out to melt cold hearts and to light up the world. As we go in the power of the Holy Spirit, we are confident that we can play our part in God's mission.

In the Eucharist, we are taken deeper into the reconciling work of Christ and go to share his unifying life (Ephesians 2:14–22). Christ has reconciled us to God and each other: our task is to actualize this truth in our homes, neighbourhoods, communities and networks. Christ said, "I, when I am lifted up from the earth, will draw all people to myself" (John 12:32). Having removed all separations and healed all divisions, Christ seeks to unite all people through us. The Church is evangelized by God and is given the task of evangelizing the world for God through its words and actions. God alone reconciles but God issues the call to enter this gift of a restored relationship with God and each other through the Church (2 Corinthians 5:20). The Church is called to preach this unchanging gospel in each generation: humanity flourishes and is fulfilled in Christ. This truth is an invitation to know God and receive God's abundant life through Christ (John 10:10).

Christianity cannot be reduced to a set of values or to moral guidance or even to a political bias to the poor. Neither a secular utopia nor a doom-laden apocalyptic grand finale is the goal of our existence or the end of history. As Creator, Redeemer, and Fulfiller, Christ is the beginning, the centre and the consummation of all that exists. In the Christian vision, creation's goal is fulfilment in Christ for "all things have been created through him and for him" (Colossians 1:16).

Living distinctively for Christ

Christianity as an intellectual thesis can be called into question. One objection is that it is incomprehensible how a good and omnipotent God can allow so much suffering in the world. This charge has some validity and crops up repeatedly in debates. The Church must engage in these intellectual arguments, while realizing rigorous discussions have their limitations and rational arguments often leave people unmoved.

The Church is an easy target for criticism. It can often be caught up in internal debate, mired in bureaucracy, and can seem reduced to rather bland public pronouncements. That may be seen as simply a fault inherent within institutions generally, as opposed to a failing of this particular institution. Yet, the Church must not be inhibited by its own divisions but be more vocal in national and international debates. The Church as a worldwide movement is well placed to speak out on global issues, such as climate change, the misery of refugees, the treatment of asylum seekers, famine, war, and the sickening chasm between the lifestyles of the mega-rich and the poorest. While praying for its own renewal, the Church cannot wait until it is beyond censure before speaking out prophetically. The Church must defend the powerless and voiceless.

Above all the world needs churches and Christians to be holy. In a rapidly changing world, churches conserve the enduring values of love, faithfulness and compassion; they continue to form strong, kind and courageous people, and they are also a stable and nourishing presence in their communities. Holy people and holy churches have an impact; they make people curious. They make people think about their own lives, their hopes and priorities. Intrigued by what they have encountered, they begin to ask questions about the life of faith and are ready to hear the good news of God's love in Jesus Christ.

The Church holds before us the vision of humanity living peacefully and justly together, in harmony with the rest of creation. The Church has a responsibility to remind us of our duty to care for those who are vulnerable, for example refugees fleeing from famine, persecution or war zones. The Church is to witness to the truth that the "good life" is marked by sacrifice and service because humanity finds its fulfilment supremely in relationships of love.[82] Both the Church as a whole and individual churches fulfil their vocation by knowing Christ, and by knowing Christ are able to represent him to the world. As it is in and through the Eucharist that Christ is known, the Eucharist is essential to God's mission.

In the Eucharist, we meet in the name of the Lord Jesus and encounter the triune God. Having met with God, we are summoned to "abide in him" (John 15:4). Our lives become informed by and imbued with

Christ's life, and witness to the difference following Christ makes. To counter the consumerism and greed that blights our modern world and jeopardizes the planet's future, we refrain from endlessly amassing possessions and aim to be wiser about what we buy. Instead of having lots of very superficial relationships, we give more time to nourishing friendships. How we spend our money, the depth of our relationships, and how our faith influences the other facets of our lives, attest to our Christian discipleship. As we are given the mind and heart of Christ, we look at situations and in relationships to discern how we can best serve others, and as our hearts pulse with Christ's love, we become generous and compassionate (Ezekiel 36:26; Philippians 2:1–11).

We embody Christ in and for the world

We enter the kingdom of God in the Eucharist and go to bear witness to God's kingdom in the world. We return to our daily rhythms and routines to reflect the light, joy, and peace of the kingdom on our faces and in our lives by embodying Christ and speaking of Christ. The famous Spanish mystic of the sixteenth century, Saint John of the Cross, referred to Christ as, " . . . the Message and the Messenger".[83] Like Christ, we are to share the good news of God's love and to be the good news of God's love too. Our lives are to convey the love of the Risen Christ who is the content of the gospel. Along similar lines, Saint Francis of Assisi is widely quoted as telling his friars, "It is no good walking anywhere to preach unless our walking is our preaching."

This identification between the message and messenger can also be understood through the following analogy. A soldier was lost in action on the battlefield in the First World War. His body could not be found and, after a few weeks, with no sign of him, he was presumed to be dead. When this news was sent to his family, he was actually being nursed back to health a long way from the battlefield. He had been blown up, and with no idea of who or where he was, he had staggered far from the front line, been found and taken to the nearby civilian hospital. His amnesia proved temporary, and over several months, he regained his strength and his awareness of who he was. Then he was ready to leave, and eventually turned up on the doorstep of his home. When his mum and dad saw him, they could not, at first, believe their eyes. They embraced him, and tears of joy flowed. No words were necessary because the message "He is alive!" was conveyed by him standing there, looking at them. The message and the messenger were identical.

The goal of our discipleship is that our lives perfectly align with Christ's life so that we are good news, as well as being those who tell the good news. When the gospel of Christ that we preach is confirmed and amplified by the gospel of our lives and our life together, our witness to Christ is attractive and effective.

As our words and actions are increasingly aligned with our profession of faith in Christ, our lives become integrated and our response to God more holistic. To live a life without holding anything back, a life identified by a wholehearted commitment to God, is to embrace Christ's life. This gradual transformation involves a letting go, a willingness to change, a dying to the past, in order to be suffused by Christ's life. Slowly but surely, we find that we are living with the right intention—to God's glory—and with the right aspiration—to deepen our dependence on God's love. This is the beautiful life, the life of great love. The beauty of love touches lives and transforms the world. In the words of Dostoevsky, "Beauty will save the world."[84]

Whatever we do, we do it in the name of Christ

Whatever work we are given to do, however extraordinary or mundane, we are to do it in the name of Christ. Our aim is to unite our work and prayer into one offering to God in the power of the Holy Spirit. When we encounter frustrations in ourselves or experience conflict with those with whom we work, we seek to be patient. Our steady perseverance, centred on our holding of the situation before Christ and his cross in our prayer, changes us and keeps open the possibility of transfiguration in the circumstances we face. Whenever our minds return to what is troubling us and we get caught up in the accompanying emotional turbulence, we are to renew our trust in God. Whatever life brings, we can, by staying close to God, continue to experience God's grace, and know God's peace.

As we press on with God, we flourish, and those around us enjoy the fruit of our faith.

The Church's ascension into the kingdom of God is the beginning of the Church's mission

It is the Church's ascension into the kingdom—its encounter with the End—in the Eucharist that is the beginning of its mission. Words from T. S. Eliot's poem "Little Gidding" are instructive: "To make an end is to make a beginning. The end is where we start from . . . ".[85] The joy we experience in the Eucharist is given to us for the world. The Church witnesses to the joy of the presence of the Risen Christ who is the hope of the world; being Christ's joy, it is unabated whatever life brings, and is beyond our understanding but within our experience.

Our plans and actions are enlivened and lifted by this joy into Christ's mission to restore the world to the Father. We invite others to celebrate with us the joy of the Risen Christ who is here, and who to know is contentment:

> . . . I have learnt to be content with whatever I have. I know what it is to have little, and I know what it is to have plenty. In any and all circumstances I have learned the secret of being well-fed and of going hungry, of having plenty and of being in need. I can do all things through him who strengthens me.
>
> *Philippians 4:11–13*

Treasuring God's creation and challenging injustice

"To strive to safeguard the integrity of creation and sustain and renew the life of the earth" is one of the Five Marks of Mission, developed by the Anglican Consultative Council and adopted by the General Synod of the Church of England in 1996. In the Eucharist, our reverence for the bread and wine is the beginning of reverence for the entire world. Understanding the world as a sacrament of God's love, we know that we are to treasure creation. We are to be passionate about caring for our planet, protecting it for this and future generations, and cherishing the rich biodiversity we see around us. In the Eucharist too, we know God's plan is to bring heaven and the created order together, centred on Christ, united in the Holy Spirit, to the glory of God.

As we see global temperatures rise to dangerous levels, humanity's relationship with the rest of the created order is under scrutiny. The following images are iconic: exhausted polar bears struggling to find icebergs on which to rest; Bangladeshi villagers watching their house sink into a turbulent river; raging fires in Australia; storms in many places wreaking havoc; and Pacific islanders facing the prospect of their nation disappearing off the face of the earth. Greta Thunberg told the World Economic Forum's Annual Meeting in Davos in January 2020, "Our house is still on fire and you're fuelling the flames."

The reduction in economic activity caused by the COVID-19 pandemic has given the planet some breathing space and presents humanity with an opportunity to rethink. We cannot continue to pursue economic growth relentlessly, and must take further and decisive steps. We need to expedite the transition to renewable sources of energy. International competition must give way to international collaboration. Political inertia must be overcome, and political action accelerated. Creation belongs to God—Christ is at its centre—and Christians are to be passionate about treasuring it.

Another one of the Five Marks of God's Mission is a commitment "to seek to transform unjust structures of society, to challenge violence of every kind and to pursue peace and reconciliation". The gross inequality in the distribution of the world's resources and the huge disparities in income are unjustifiable. For example, Monaco, described as the playground of the rich, stands in staggering contrast with Malawi, where three quarters of the population have a daily income of less than two US dollars. In our global village, we can no longer plead ignorance.

The Eucharist is a subversive act, calling into question all the injustices of our world. As everyone receives the bread and wine on equal terms, the disparities of wealth and opportunity embedded in the status quo are undercut. In our coming together as children of God in the light of God's kingdom, all other loyalties are relativized and any ranking based on work, status, wealth or educational attainment is undermined: we are all on the same footing before God. This new order of God's kingdom forces us to challenge the systems that result in a vast chasm between the rich and the poor, between those who waste food and those who are wasted because they have no food.

Those who are hungry cannot be far from our minds as we eat and drink together in the Eucharist. We are, after all, food-dependent creatures looking to God to provide. Every time we sit down to eat, we know that God gives the food to eat through the work of others. This interdependence—we rely on others for the food on our plate—suggests a wider responsibility to each other: the food derived from the soil of the earth is to be shared. Thus, every meal reminds us of this duty: we are to feed the hungry. Sometimes this is alluded to in the grace before meals, for instance in the phrase: ". . . make us ever mindful of the needs of others".

With the growing gap between rich and poor, and the continuing spectre of famine and hunger in many places, the Church is summoned to pray and protest. The dissonance between how the world is and how the world should be compels the Church to speak out, to offer prophetic insight into where humanity "fall[s] short of the glory of God" (Romans 3:23). The Church's task is to critique the structures and systems that produce such staggering injustice and challenge those who hold the levers of power. The Church seeks to find a place to agitate and work most effectively for the world's transformation.[86] God's mission is urgent; it is local and global, all-enveloping; the goal is the renewal of the created order; and it is Christ's and it is ours.

In the Eucharist, having seen the wounds of Christ and received the Holy Spirit, we are sent out. Like those first disciples in the Upper Room on that first Easter Sunday, we hear Christ say to us, "As the Father has sent me, so I send you."[87] Then we go in peace and love, in the name of Christ.

Prayer

God alone can give faith
But you can give your witness.
God alone can give hope
But you can give confidence to your brothers.
God alone can give love
But you can teach others how to love.
God alone can give peace
But you can sow unity.
God alone can give strength
But you can stand by someone who is discouraged.
God alone is the way
But you can point it out to others.
God alone is the light
But you can make it shine in the eyes of all.
God alone is the life
But you can give others the will to live.
God alone can do what seems impossible
But you will be able to do what is possible.
God alone is sufficient for himself
But he prefers to count on you.

Team of Campinas (Brazil)[88]

EPILOGUE

The Eucharist in a time of pandemic

Rejoice in hope, be patient in suffering, persevere in prayer.
Romans 12:12

Colin, the head of the monastery at Crawley Down, wrote to me during the lockdown caused by the COVID-19 pandemic, "We are able to keep up the Eucharist conscious that this is a privilege at the moment, and hope that this is our small contribution." With churches closed, he knew how special it was still to be celebrating the Eucharist.

There have been many thoughtful responses to churches being closed, aimed at helping Christians maintain and strengthen their discipleship. One of these is "spiritual communion", a practice for anyone who is prevented from receiving the Eucharist. These prayers have a strong sense of personal devotion to Jesus, and the central plea is that Jesus comes into our hearts. This confidence in the closeness of Jesus is based on our baptism, which is the guarantee of our communion with him, assuring us that, even when we are unable to celebrate the Eucharist, we continue to know him. Besides encountering him in our prayers, we meet him in our everyday lives, in the people we meet, and the opportunities and challenges we face. "Spiritual communion" is a springboard into seeing every aspect and our total existence as spiritual, a way of relating to God who is love.

Churches have risen to the challenge of offering prayers to be said at home and online services. This worship has been appreciated and been well-attended, attracting many not accustomed to going to church. Those who have internet access and are computer savvy can join relatively easily to sample the worship or stay for the entire service. Those who find crossing a church's threshold daunting, and people who are housebound, have valued the opportunity to access services at home. This might well lead to churches continuing to broadcast online beyond lockdown, but we must not lose sight of those who cannot use the internet.

Others have regarded their deprivation of the Eucharist as a fast, a discipline for this season. "Fasting from the Eucharist" is adopted by many churches on Good Friday when, to identify with Jesus' desolation at Calvary, Christians deny themselves this consolation. For those unable to celebrate the Eucharist in lockdown, their impoverishment could be seen as a further opportunity to relate to the anguish of Jesus' crucifixion, and the agony of those struggling and suffering because of coronavirus, locally and globally.

Like the community at Crawley Down, Christians elsewhere who have been able to celebrate the Eucharist have been profoundly aware of those denied this gift. Their awareness that the Eucharist is prayed on behalf of those who cannot assemble has helped to allay this disquiet. Although the Eucharist is a personal joy, it is offered to God for the Church and the world, and its scope includes those present and those absent. Eucharists held in enclosed communities, and in some households where a resident has led the service, have all been a contribution to the Church's life, and the delight of those able to celebrate, along with the grief of those who cannot, has been offered to God.

There has also been reflection on the merits of online eucharistic services when only those in the same location as the individual leading the celebration can receive the bread and wine. Those unable to attend in person can only watch as those present receive the body and blood of Christ, and can at that point be labelled "spectators", but everyone participates in every other aspect of the service. Our discipleship is strengthened as we are penitent, hear the Ministry of the Word, respond through the Creed and intercessions, share the Peace, join in with the great prayer of thanksgiving, call together on the Father, and recommit ourselves to love and serve God. Sharing in a eucharistic celebration, even though we cannot eat the body and drink the blood of Christ, still deepens our faith, strengthens our resolve to follow Christ, and includes our prayers for the Church and the world.

There has been some discussion too about whether a way can be found for those who join Eucharists online to receive consecrated bread and wine. One option mooted is for those participating from afar to have bread and wine with them, and for the president to intend to include these separated elements in different places in the one central prayer. No consensus has emerged, but one of the obstacles has been the sense that this would make the Eucharist disjointed, with those physically present and those present online having different experiences. Though together in time, the online congregation would be fragmented in space. The contemporaneous experience is undermined by the participants being physically distanced from each other. There cannot be a common cup or one loaf to share, and the consecration cannot happen in one place. This lack of commonality detracts from the Eucharist's integrity, and its unifying function in the life of the Church.

Discussions about how the Eucharist might be celebrated online have also highlighted the importance of the relationship between the participants. Whereas the ease of access to the service through the internet means that people can participate from across the globe, there does not have to be a relationship between the participants. An open invitation is, of course, a defining characteristic of any Christian community and, in any church service, there can be people who are exploring faith, are relatively new or are attending for the first time. Yet, they are physically together, bound at least by close proximity, and can relate to each other face to face. To that extent, everyone is known. Also, most churches recognize the link between receiving the body and blood of Christ and discipleship, and have guidelines about who can receive the body and blood of Christ. Unless the participants are known, it is hard to see how this practice can be upheld.

The kingdom of God, the Eucharist and the pandemic

In the Eucharist, we stand as equals before God, loved and cherished. We pray together, "Our Father ... your kingdom come, your will be done on earth as in heaven." This experience of God's all-embracing love and the longing for the kingdom at the heart of the Lord's Prayer shapes the Church's mission, and puts the quest for justice at its heart.

The COVID-19 pandemic has highlighted the inequalities that blight our nation and the world. The disparities in the quality of people's lives have come to the fore. In lockdown, those cooped up in flats have faced a far greater challenge than those living in large houses with a garden. There is a correlation between the risk of dying from COVID-19 and poor health, which in turn is linked to poverty. When we gaze around the world, those living in cramped conditions in shanty towns and refugee camps have been disturbingly vulnerable, effectively trapped and exposed to the virus.

This crisis has elicited some positive responses too. The profile of those working in hospitals, in care homes, in retail and in public transport has been raised, and they have known society's gratitude as they have gone on working. Those living on the streets have been given accommodation. There have been many individual acts of kindness, and faith-based bodies and other agencies have rallied together to support those who are struggling.

In the Eucharist, we know God's vision of a just and peaceful world. The view from the kingdom of God compels us to serve those who are poor and powerless, and to strive for a better world. This has been seen in churches' responses to need in their locality. In Birmingham where I live many churches have been involved in food distribution through their own local initiatives and through food banks, working with other voluntary organizations and the city council. Alongside offering practical help, churches have also offered pastoral and emotional support to those who are lonely, those whose domestic situation is distressing, and those whose mental health has deteriorated during lockdown. The constant call to God's people to shape a better world has been met creatively and confidently.

Loss, lament and the Eucharist

The eventual number of deaths worldwide from COVID-19 is going to be measured in hundreds of thousands, if not millions. Each individual death is hard to bear for those close to the deceased, and some families have seen multiple deaths. In the UK, the black, Asian and minority ethnic (BAME) community has been disproportionately affected. Certain professions have been hit hard: doctors, nurses, care workers and bus drivers, for example. This colossal loss of life calls for lament, a tear-soaked expression of our collective grief.

This sense of dislocation has prompted a search for biblical analogies. Kept away from our sacred spaces, we can draw a parallel with God's people in exile in Babylon when they cried in distress, "How could we sing the Lord's song in a foreign land?" (Psalm 137:4).

Our grief in this time of waiting makes Easter Saturday instructive for us. Then first followers of Jesus were bereft. With his death, their shared life had been ruptured. Life felt empty; the future uncertain. Yet, the dawning of the new day heralded the resurrection of Christ.

The supreme place for reflection is the Paschal Mystery. Gazing at the cross, we see God's solidarity with those who suffer and God's inexhaustible love. The Risen Christ is the proclamation of God's faithfulness, even in death; love is stronger than death. This truth can give comfort and hope to those who mourn. This dynamic of resurrection following death raises the prospect that out of this catastrophic loss of life, a more just and compassionate world might emerge. As this pandemic has once more underlined humanity's interdependence, we pray that it may lead to a new era of international collaboration to address the many global challenges we face, and to ensure the world is better prepared for any future health crisis. For the Church, there has been a renewed summons to practical service of our neighbour and our local community, and a return to a central truth of our faith: God is love, and we love God by loving each other. Even though the Eucharist has not been celebrated in our churches, eucharistic living has been a notable feature of the churches' response to lockdown: the Church has continued to rejoice, to give thanks and to share God's love.

Prayer

Risen Christ,
Hold us in our isolation,
Comfort us in our grief,
Heal us in our sickness,
Calm us in our anxiety,
Be light in our darkness.
Energise us in your service,
And give us patience as we wait
to meet you in the breaking of the bread.
Amen.

Bibliography

Anonymous, *The Cloud of Unknowing and the Book of Privy Counselling*, edited by William Johnston (New York; Image books, 1973).

Behr, John, *The Mystery of Christ* (Yonkers, NY: St Vladimir Press, 2006).

Book of Common Prayer (Cambridge: Cambridge University Press, 1987).

Bouyer, Louis, *A History of Christian Spirituality*, Volume 1 (Tunbridge Wells: Burns and Oates, 1982).

Bouyer, Louis, *Eucharist* (South Bend, IN: University of Notre Dame Press, 1989).

Brother Lawrence, *The Practice of the Presence of God* (Oxford: Mowbray, 1980).

Caussade, J. P. de, *Abandonment to Divine Providence*, translated by Kelly Muggeridge (London: Fount, 1981).

Celebrating Common Prayer (London: Mowbray, 1992).

Clarke, S., *The Marrow of Ecclesiastical History, Life of Queen Elizabeth* (1675).

Community of the Servants of the Will of God, *Vespers, Dedication Festival of the Chape*, (Crawley Down: CSWG, 2019).

Common Worship (main volume) (London: Church House Publishing, 2000).

Common Worship: Initiation Services (London: Church House Publishing, 2000).

Common Worship: Pastoral Services (London: Church House Publishing, 2000).

Davison, Andrew, *Blessing* (Norwich: Canterbury Press, 2014).

Diamond, John, C., *Because Cowards get Cancer Too* (London: Vermillion, 1998).

Dillistone, F. W., *The Power of Symbols* (London: SCM Press, 1986).

Donovan, Vincent, *Christianity Rediscovered* (London: SCM Press, 1982).

Dostoevsky, Fyodor, *The Idiot* (Ware, Hertfordshire: Wordsworth, 1996).

Eliot, T. S., *Four Quartets* (London: Faber & Faber, 1959).
Foster, Richard, *Celebration of Discipline* (London: Hodder & Stoughton, 1980).
Galbreath, Paul, *Leading from the Table* (Herndon, VA: The Alban Institute, 2008).
Gardner, Helen (ed.), *Religious Verse* (London: Faber & Faber Ltd, 1979).
Gasper, Julia, *Elizabeth Craven: Writer, Feminist and European* (Malaga, Spain: Vernon Press, 2017).
Herbert Christopher (ed.), *Pocket Prayers* (London, Church House Publishing, 1993).
Hopkins, Gerard Manley, *Poems and Prose* (London: Penguin, 1985).
Howard, Geoffrey, *Dare to Break Bread* (London: Darton, Longman and Todd, 1992).
Leech, Kenneth, *True God: An Exploration in Spiritual Theology* (London: Sheldon Press, 1985).
Leech, Kenneth, *True Prayer: An Invitation to Christian Spirituality* (London: Sheldon Press, 1980).
Lossky, Vladimir, *The Mystical Theology of the Eastern Church* (Cambridge: James Clarke, 1991).
Merton, Thomas, *Confessions of a Guilty Bystander* (New York: Doubleday, 1966).
Miller, James, *Praying the Eucharist* (London: SPCK, 1995).
Moltmann, Jürgen, *The Open Church: Invitation to an Open Messianic Lifestyle* (London: SPCK, 1978).
Perham, Michael, *Lively Sacrifice* (London: SPCK, 1992).
Pseudo-Dionysius, *Complete Works* (London: SPCK, 1987).
Quiller-Couch, Sir Arthur (ed.), *The Oxford Book of English Verse 1250–1918* (Oxford: Clarendon Press, 1939).
Ramsey, Michael, *The Gospel and the Catholic Church* (London: SPCK, 1990).
Ramsey, Michael, *The Anglican Spirit* (Boston, MA: Cowley, 1991).
Sachs, Oliver, *Gratitude* (New York: Random House, 2015).
Schmemann, Alexander, *The Eucharist* (Crestwood, NY: St. Vladimir's Seminary Press, 1987).
Schmemann, Alexander, *For the Life of the World* (Crestwood, NY: St. Vladimir's Seminary Press, 1988).

Thomas, R. S., *The Bright Field: Laboratories of the Spirit* (New York: MacMillan, 1975).

Tillard, J.-M. R., *Church of Churches* (Collegeville, MN: Liturgical Press, 1992).

Underhill, Evelyn, *The Mystery of Sacrifice* (Wilton, CT: Morehouse Publishing, 1991).

Vanstone, W. H., *Love's Endeavour, Love's Expense* (London: Darton, Longman and Todd, 1977).

Varden, Eric, *The Shattering of Loneliness* (London: Bloomsbury Continuum, 2018).

Vanier, Jean, *Community and Growth* (London: Darton, Longman and Todd, 2001).

Wilkinson, David, *When I pray what does God do?* (Oxford: Monarch Books, 2015).

Williams, Rowan, *Resurrection* (London: SPCK, 2002).

Williams, Rowan, *Being Christian* (London: SPCK, 2014).

Williams, Rowan, *Being Disciples* (London: SPCK, 2016).

Williams, Rowan, *God with Us* (London: SPCK, 2017).

Williams, Rowan, *Christ—the Heart of Creation* (London: Bloomsbury, 2018).

Notes

1. Interview in the *Guardian* on 27 January 2020.
2. Anonymous, *The Cloud of Unknowing*, Chapter 6, in *The Cloud of Unknowing and the Book of Privy Counselling*, William Johnston (ed.), (New York; Image books, 1973), p. 54.
3. Kenneth Leech, *True Prayer* (London: Sheldon Press, 1980), p. 153.
4. Leech, *True Prayer*, pp. 36–7.
5. *Common Worship* (main volume) (London: Church House Publishing, 2000), p. 32.
6. *Celebrating Common Prayer* (London: Mowbray 1992), p. 145.
7. For more of John's story, see John Diamond, *C: Because Cowards Get Cancer Too* (London: Vermillion, 1998).
8. Helen Gardner (ed.), *Religious Verse* (London: Faber & Faber Ltd, 1979), p. 97.
9. Second Collect for Peace at Morning Prayer, *Book of Common Prayer* (Cambridge: Cambridge University Press, 1987), p. 13.
10. Fred R. Shapiro, *"Who wrote the Serenity Prayer?"* (Washington, D.C.: The Chronicle of Higher Education, 2014).
11. Fyodor Dostoevsky, *The Idiot* (Ware, Hertfordshire: Wordsworth, 1996), p. 204.
12. Herbert Christopher (ed.), *Pocket Prayers* (London, Church House Publishing, 1993), p. 27.
13. Quote from *Time Magazine*, published on Friday, 31 May 1963.
14. *Common Worship* (main volume), p. 190.
15. Herbert (ed.), *Pocket Prayers*, p. 14.
16. The quote is from a sermon preached at the morning mass at the Vatican on 23 May 2016.
17. Community of the Servants of the Will of God, *Vespers, Dedication Festival of the Chapel*, (Crawley Down: CSWG, 2019), p. 2.

18. This phrase is the last line of the final verse of the hymn "Love divine, all loves excelling" by Charles Wesley.
19. *Common Worship* (main volume), p. 291.
20. Evelyn Underhill, *The Mystery of Sacrifice* (Wilton, CT: Morehouse Publishing, 1991), p. 20.
21. Elizabeth Craven, in Julia Gasper, *Elizabeth Craven: Writer, Feminist and European* (Malaga, Spain: Vernon Press, 2017), p. 269–70.
22. Romans 6:3; 1 Corinthians 10:17; 12:13.
23. Kenneth Leech, *True God* (London: Sheldon Press, 1985) p. 258.
24. *Common Worship* ((main volume), p. 182.
25. "The waiting Father" is a reference to the father in the parable of the Prodigal Son (Luke 15:11–32).
26. "Lover of humanity" as a referent for God in the Orthodox tradition.
27. *Religious Verse*, p. 288.
28. R. S. Thomas, *The Bright Field: Laboratories of the Spirit* (New York: MacMillan, 1975), p. 60.
29. W. H. Davies' poem "Leisure" in Sir Arthur Quiller-Couch (ed.), *The Oxford Book of English Verse 1250–1918*, (Oxford: Clarendon Press, 1939), p. 1101.
30. A variation on the Church of England wedding vows in *Common Worship: Pastoral Services* (London: Church House Publishing, 2000), p. 108.
31. Derived from the Church of England vows at the exchange of the wedding rings in *Common Worship: Pastoral Services*, p. 109.
32. *Religious verse*, p. 132.
33. Thomas Merton, *Confessions of a Guilty Bystander* (New York: Doubleday, 1966), p. 140.
34. Matthew 26:29; Mark 14:22; Luke 22:30.
35. Line is from Edith Sitwell's poem, "Eurydice", and is the title of *An Anthology for those who Grieve*, edited by Agnes Whitaker (London: Darton, Longman and Todd, 1984).
36. Isaiah 25:6–9, 49:9, 65:13; Ezekiel 34:25–30.
37. Collect for the eighteenth Sunday after Trinity, *Common Worship*, p. 419.
38. Introductory words to the liturgy of the Eucharist—see *Common Worship*, p. 167.
39. Phrase "angels and archangels and with all the company of heaven" taken from Eucharistic Prayer B in *Common Worship* (main volume), p. 188.
40. *Common Worship* (main volume), p. 176.

41   "Gather Us In" by Marty Haugen, © 1982, GIA Publications, Inc. All rights reserved. Used by permission.
42   Bible reference for the Parable of the Waiting Father, also known as the Parable of the Prodigal Son, is Luke 15:11–32.
43   "Worth it" is a reference to a L'Oréal campaign with the strapline, "Because you're worth it".
44   Brother Lawrence, *The Practice of the Presence of God* (Oxford: Mowbray, 1980), p. 50.
45   "Just as I am" is a reference to the hymn of the same name by Charlotte Elliott.
46   *Common Worship* (main volume), p. 168.
47   The final lines of hymn "When I survey the wondrous cross" by Isaac Watts.
48   Leech, *True God*, p. 302, quoting Karl Barth.
49   *Celebrating Common Prayer*, p. 244.
50   *Common Worship* (main volume), p. 171.
51   *Common Worship* (main volume), p. 188.
52   Isaiah 49:6; Matthew 5:14; John 8:12.
53   Psalm 95:8–9; Matthew 4:1–11; Luke 4:1–13.
54   John Behr, *Mystery of Christ* (Yonkers, NY: St Vladimir Press, 2006), p. 167.
55   Underhill, *Mystery of Sacrifice*, p. 24.
56   Acts 2:38; 3:19,26; 5:31; 17:30; 26:20.
57   Collect for the last Sunday after Trinity, *Common Worship*, p. 422.
58   *Common Worship* (main volume), p. 173.
59   *Pseudo-Dionysius: Complete Works* (London: SPCK, 1987), pp. 217–8.
60   Herbert, *Pocket Prayers*, p. 37.
61   David Wilkinson, *When I pray what does God do?* (Oxford: Monarch Books, 2015), p. 96.
62   A quote from his "Remaining Awake Through a Great Revolution" speech, given at the National Cathedral on 31 March 1968.
63   Underhill, *Mystery of Sacrifice*, p. 32.
64   Underhill, *Mystery of Sacrifice*, p. 32.
65   Herbert, *Pocket Prayers*, p. 35.
66   *Common Worship* (main volume), p. 290.
67   Luke 6:32–6; John 13:1–7; Romans 15:1–7; 2 Corinthians 5:14; Colossians 3:13.
68   Matthew 28:16–20; Philippians 2:9; Ephesians 1:10.

69 Vincent Donovan, *Christianity Rediscovered* (London: SCM Press, 1982), pp. 60–1.
70 Herbert, *Pocket Prayers,* p. 82.
71 *Common Worship* (main volume), p. 188.
72 *Common Worship* (main volume), pp. 188–90.
73 S. Clarke, *The Marrow of Ecclesiastical History, Life of Queen Elizabeth* (1675), pt. 2, bk. 1 *The Life of Queen Elizabeth.*
74 *Celebrating Common Prayer,* p. 183.
75 Rowan Williams, *Being Christian* (London: SPCK, 2014), p. 70.
76 Kenneth Leech, *True Prayer,* p. 22.
77 *Common Worship* (main volume), p. 178.
78 Taken from the first verse of the hymn "Guide me, O thou great redeemer" by William Williams, translated from the Welsh by Peter Williams.
79 Matthew 15:32–9; Mark 6:30–44; Luke 9:12–17; John 6:1–15.
80 *Common Worship* (main volume), p. 182.
81 *Common Worship* (main volume), p. 183.
82 The saying the "good life" was first coin by the philosopher Aristotle in the fourth century BCE.
83 Underhill, *Mystery of Sacrifice,* p. 67.
84 Dostoevsky, *The Idiot,* p. 356.
85 T. S. Eliot, *Four Quartets* (London: Faber & Faber, 1959), p. 47.
86 Cf. Archimedes' "Give me a place to stand and with a lever, I will move the whole world."
87 John 20:21.
88 J.-M. R. Tillard, *Church of Churches* (Collegeville, MN: Liturgical Press, 1992), p. 252.

EU GPSR Authorized Representative:

LOGOS EUROPE, 9 rue Nicolas Poussin, 17000 La Rochelle, France

contact@logoseurope.eu

www.ingramcontent.com/pod-product-compliance
Lightning Source LLC
Chambersburg PA
CBHW070552160426
43199CB00014B/2468